the BECKONING

What People Are Saying About *The Beckoning*

Encouraging to fellow believers and a revelation to skeptics, Michael Minot's recounting of how he was wooed from atheism to faith is a fascinating read, unique in its approach and thorough in its layout of his case.

—**Jerry B. Jenkins**, Writer of the *Left Behind* series

An amazing story and superbly written. *The Beckoning* may be one of the most powerful conversion stories brought to print in the last 10 years. Page after page, so many insights I never considered before. And I've been a Christ follower for more than 40 years. An outstanding read.

—**Dr. Larry Thompson**, Senior Pastor,
First Baptist Church of Fort Lauderdale, Florida

A fascinating look from the inside at the probing mind of a skilled attorney. Rarely does one find so many fresh perspectives and unique insights in one book. For anyone exploring matters of faith, *The Beckoning* is a must-read."

—**Hugh Jones**, Attorney and Executive Director, Charity Counsel

The Beckoning may be one of the most clear and direct perspectives on God and His Kingdom that I've ever read. The way each chapter builds to the final explanation of God's ultimate plan kept me turning the pages as fast as I could. As a pastor for many years, I was astonished at how much I learned about God's character after reading this powerful book.

—**Dr. Erick Brookins**, Senior Pastor,
Surfside Community Church, Port Saint John, Florida

Few books possess the power to radically change your life. This book may be one of them.

—**Eric Curtis**, COO, Christian Associates International

Through our ministry we encounter students around the world who are hungry for solid answers to life's big questions. In a practical and engaging way, Michael offers critical insights to these issues by bringing to life the truths that led him to the stunning conclusion that he's a created being. My hope is that every student reads this fantastic book.

—**David Eaton**, CEO, Axis Ministries

People of the 21st century church are in dire need of understanding the unchanging truths of Christianity in a way that empowers them to share those truths with an ever changing culture. *The Beckoning* beautifully portrays what Michael discovered while attempting to disprove the claims that God is real. This book should hold a prominent place in every believer's library.

—**Rich Griffith**, Former NFL Football Player,
Pastor, Woodmen Valley Chapel, Colorado Springs, Colorado

Intelligent, yet plainly and clearly written. This unique, thought-provoking book reveals the inner thoughts, fears, and prejudices of an atheist attorney trying to substantiate his views. But in the end, something entirely unexpected happens...

—**Steven Martens**, Chief of Staff (Ret.), Greater Europe Mission

Compelling and provocative. Whether a follower of Christ, a prodigal, or a skeptic, anyone searching for a better understanding of life and truth should read this sensational book. *The Beckoning* is a great resource for small groups as well as those wanting to start conversations with skeptical family members and friends.

—**Peter Lord**, Senior Pastor (Ret.),
Park Avenue Baptist Church, Titusville Florida

All humans want respect and dignity. What I love about this book is that Michael speaks with dignity to those who are searching. You'll appreciate the opportunity to peer over Michael's shoulder as he examines the evidence for God and the implications of faith. If you're a believer, you'll be strengthened and encouraged. Michael's journey will inspire you and challenge you to a deeper level of commitment.

—**Dr. Sid Webb**, President, Sharpened Focus LLC

Intellectually speaking, becoming a follower of God has just become a whole lot easier. This is a story of one atheist who pushed himself to honestly and critically evaluate the evidence for and against the existence of God. Every student desperately needs to read this book.

—**Rick Schenker**, President, Ratio Christi Ministries

the
BECKONING

*Examining the Truths
That Transformed an Atheist Attorney
Into a Believer In God*

Michael Minot

NEW YORK

the BECKONING

Examining the Truths That Transformed an Atheist Attorney Into a Believer In God

Published in New York, New York, by Morgan James Publishing. Morgan James and The Entrepreneurial Publisher are trademarks of Morgan James, LLC. www.MorganJamesPublishing.com

The Morgan James Speakers Group can bring authors to your live event. For more information or to book an event visit The Morgan James Speakers Group at www.TheMorganJamesSpeakersGroup.com.

Unless otherwise noted, Scripture references taken from the Holy Bible, New International Version®, NIV® Copyright © 1973, 1978, 1984, 2011 by Biblica, Inc.® Used by permission. All rights reserved worldwide. Scripture also taken from: New King James Version (NKJV)

The Holy Bible, New King James Version Copyright © 1982 by Thomas Nelson, Inc. Living Bible (TLB) The Living Bible copyright © 1971 by Tyndale House Foundation. Used by permission of Tyndale House Publishers Inc., Carol Stream, Illinois 60188. All rights reserved. English Standard Version (ESV) The Holy Bible, English Standard Version Copyright © 2001 by Crossway Bibles, a division of Good News Publishers.

A free eBook edition is available with the purchase of this print book.

ISBN 978-1-63047-124-8 paperback
ISBN 978-1-63047-125-5 eBook
ISBN 978-1-63047-126-2 hardcover
Library of Congress Control Number:
2014933863

CLEARLY PRINT YOUR NAME ABOVE IN UPPER CASE

Instructions to claim your free eBook edition:
1. Download the BitLit app for Android or iOS
2. Write your name in **UPPER CASE** on the line
3. Use the BitLit app to submit a photo
4. Download your eBook to any device

Cover Design by:
Rachel Lopez
www.r2cdesign.com

Interior Design by:
Bonnie Bushman
bonnie@caboodlegraphics.com

In an effort to support local communities, raise awareness and funds, Morgan James Publishing donates a percentage of all book sales for the life of each book to Habitat for Humanity Peninsula and Greater Williamsburg.

Get involved today, visit
www.MorganJamesBuilds.com

Habitat for Humanity®
Peninsula and
Greater Williamsburg
Building Partner

*This book is dedicated
to all those pursuing truth.*

TABLE OF CONTENTS

PREFACE

I'm often asked to describe what happened during the months I spent researching these issues. They want to know what facts were so persuasive that an atheist attorney would become a believer in God. But I never felt I could respond in a way that told the true story. No short answer seemed sufficient. So now, in the following pages, I'll describe for the first time the specifics of what jolted me out of my atheism.

—Michael Minot

MY STORY: FROM ATHEISM TO FAITH

To view Michael's introductory video for Chapter 1,
please go to www.michaelminot.com/thebeckoning.

hakespeare wrote in *As You Like It*, "All the world is a stage and all the men and women merely players." For a good chunk of my early life I lived by this philosophy. Refusing to waste my time entertaining absurd impossibilities, I firmly rejected Christianity. Instead, I focused on becoming a top tier "player" and claiming my share of what the world offered.

But several years after graduating from law school, my freethinking, anti-religious convictions collapsed. After more than three months of reading books, articles, and the Scriptures and engaging in some very serious introspection, the truth I discovered devastated my skepticism. I came to realize that my atheistic philosophy failed miserably against the strength of God's truth. Humbled to my core, I told God I wanted everything He offered. I further indicated my desire to say "yes" to anything He wanted me to do.

Of course, this dramatic shift in my beliefs didn't occur instantly.

I remember a time early in life when my curiosity seemed limitless. I always wanted to know more. Most of all, nature fascinated me. I asked questions of my parents and teachers like: "How do bees make their hives?" "Why do caterpillars turn into butterflies?" "Where do all the colors on flowers come from?" Something about the beauty of nature and my ability to look up and see the moon and the stars amazed me.

One of the more memorable moments of my childhood occurred as I was walking outside just before bedtime on a humid, Florida summer night when I was nine years old. My upward gaze was fixed with wonder on the bright light coming from the moon. A few days earlier, I'd witnessed three astronauts blaze a trail into the atmosphere on what looked like a pillar of fire coming from nearby Kennedy Space Center. But despite knowing their mission, I wasn't prepared for the utter amazement of the moment. Just before walking outside, I heard Neil Armstrong utter these profound words on television, "One small step for man. One giant leap for mankind." Stepping outside, I wondered, *How can a man walk on the moon? How can someone be standing on what I was staring at in the nighttime sky?*

Exploring Success

Somewhere on the way to adulthood, however, I lost my wide-eyed fascination with nature and the stars. My newly-acquired desire for success and a craving for what the world offered began suffocating my curiosity and choking out my childlike wonder.

As I entered adolescence, I began seeing the world as a place where the strongest prosper. Success seemed to follow those who committed themselves to becoming the best at something. I ended up choosing tennis as my first venture at becoming one of the best. Throughout my teenage years, I trained for and attended state and national junior tennis tournaments year-round. As I suspected, the payoffs made the hard work well worth it. My passion for tennis brought me notoriety, the ability to travel, and the opportunity to attend college on an athletic scholarship.

During my time in college, whether preparing for a test, training for tennis competitions, or eventually earning a law degree, life for me consisted of a consuming series of short-term goals. I was intent on staying busy and focused. But all my goal-oriented activities consumed me so completely that I neglected to pause and ponder life's most important questions.

Throughout my teenage and early adult years, my "go-getter" attitude stood in stark contrast to how I addressed the issues surrounding the purpose of living. With little questioning, I accepted what my professors and peers suggested was the meaning of life. I held the opinion that humans live without guidance from any outside source. To me, life was whatever I made it and nothing else. As a consequence, I made it my business every day to get all I could while I could.

But as I reflect back on that time of my life, I realize that although believing myself to be wise, I was foolish. My atheistic convictions had blinded me to any competing views of life. Even when people around me described the truth, I didn't listen. Filled with a closed-minded attitude, I failed to realize how desperately I needed help.

A New Discovery

After wrapping up law school, I set out to reap the rewards of all my hard work. Soon, I was living the American dream—money in my pocket, the keys to a new convertible, and a keen desire to socialize.

But a few years later while vigorously pursuing the fruits that came from my professional abilities, I received a call from a friend I'd met years earlier while studying for the Florida bar exam. Seeing where my life was heading, he suggested that this might be a good time for me to take a step back and reevaluate the meaning of my life. He went on to explain how at one point he reviewed the Scriptures and how they became of an important part of his life. He went on to say that I might benefit from listening to a highly respected Christian pastor he knew in my area.

After the conversation ended, I was startled that my friend would even make these suggestions. The trajectory of my life was going up at a steep angle. To me, life was great—beyond my dreams—and getting better all the time. Why should I spend time considering anything else? What could be the benefit of seeking answers to questions I wasn't asking?

But with the time pressures of formal education behind me and living alone, I recognized my friend's invitation came at a unique period in my life. Possibly unlike any other time, I could do as my friend suggested and reevaluate the big picture of my life. The most likely outcome, I thought, was that I would confirm my disbelief while gaining ammunition to support my views. With these thoughts in mind I called my friend back and accepted his challenge.

As with anything else I took up in life, I didn't want my investigation to be a half-baked effort. So, I not only acquired a copy of the Scriptures and other related material, but I added another area of inquiry. To be thorough and fair, I knew the issues raised by science needed a fresh and fair investigation as well.

My Personal Reckoning

Unfortunately, when I began my research, I recognized a problem. I realized that my perception of how life worked was so ingrained it was preventing me from being objective. I was forced to concede that my thoughts were not being guided by what I was reading, but rather by my firm belief that everything has a natural explanation, not a supernatural one.

At this point, I remembered a promise I made to myself years earlier. I vowed never to turn away from a truth that was staring me in the face. No matter how uncomfortable, I pledged to incorporate and live by whatever truth I discovered. I didn't want to be the type of person who avoided the truth in favor of living some self-deluded, pretend life.

Considering this, I made up my mind rather easily about how to handle this dilemma. I knew that if I didn't adopt a neutral attitude, my investigation would be a waste of time. So, knowing that it might be easier said than done, I pledged to maintain an open mind and go wherever the evidence led. From that moment on, I did my best to critically examine everything I was reading.

Amazing Discoveries

With my resolve to maintain an objective attitude firmly in place, I resumed my reading of the Scriptures as well as various articles and books on science and philosophy. To my shock and amazement, it wasn't long before I began discovering statements so profound I couldn't continue reading without pausing to ponder their vast significance. One by one, newly discovered truths began hammering a wedge into the thick wall of my prejudices. Night after night, I continued to study, reevaluating the world around me as I went. After more than two months, I must have looked like an awestruck research scientist as I paced around my house muttering things like, "It just can't be!"

Towards the end of my investigation I found myself facing a massive mosaic of evidence that I'd never considered before. Despite my extreme cynicism, the evidence I'll be sharing with you in this book began to overwhelm me. A short time later, after more than three months of study and careful consideration of everything I'd learned, I did the unthinkable: I broke down and concluded it was more likely than not that *I was a created being!* And just like that, the pillars supporting how I viewed the world and myself began to collapse.

As I read and reread various books and articles on science, I began to recognize the amazing precision found in nature. From the material I read on modern-day astronomy, to the amazing world being unlocked by microbiology, I discovered an astonishing order that tied all things together. I found it difficult not to conclude that some Master Architect or Engineer was behind all the complementary systems I was reading about.

I was amazed to learn how the Scriptures read like a lengthy love letter from the Creator to the objects of His love. Sometimes they issued stern warnings. But their underlying message is one of deep, unconditional love. I could've easily defended against a series of do's and don'ts or a disconnected series of suggestions about how best to live life. But I had little defense for how the Bible integrates with such perfection and detail the description of who we are along with God's plan for our lives. I never read a more remarkable, comprehensive story. I began to realize that what God provides—including everything in our surroundings—invites us to a most wonderful life that only begins here on earth.

I arrived at the conclusion that not only is it possible for us to know, but in fact we are made to know, how God offers His ongoing love to each of us. Whether seen or unseen, understood fully or not, everything that exists serves to provoke mankind to the truth that He is our Creator. I learned that God delivers His invitation in a multitude of ways, each working in conjunction with the others. Through this, as we will see in the upcoming pages, He attempts to arouse within us a desire to investigate His immeasurable love.

The change in my perspective caused dramatic repercussions. Nothing was remotely the same even though the only thing that changed was me. I felt like I'd been awakened into a whole new existence.

Wrestling with Tough Questions

After I became a new Christian I wanted to learn more. I also desired to celebrate my beliefs with others who followed God. So, I joined a church. I assumed when I connected with others who believed the Scriptures that they would share the same joy I'd found. But ironically, I discovered that I was traveling a path opposite to many church goers. I learned that some in the church, especially teens and young adults, were confused by various aspects of their faith. More than a few were so frustrated that they were abandoning their childhood beliefs altogether.

I later discovered that young adults are leaving the church in unprecedented numbers.[1] But why are they leaving? Some teenagers have told me that the information they receive from their parents and youth group leaders is too elementary and repetitive. They say the church offers messages that don't relate to their experiences in life. Some receive the discouraging response, "You simply need to have more faith!"

Without understanding how the Scriptures fit into everyday life, many adolescents and young adults label what they were taught as either not relevant to their lives—or worse, outright fairy tales. Because they cannot connect the dots between the church's message and everything they see and experience, their interest in faith wanes. After waiting for answers that never come, belief gives way to skepticism.

Along the way, I've also found that some in the middle and later years of life find their once resilient faith weakening too. Why are some of God's followers not finishing life well?

A Few Personal Conclusions

These experiences along with my involvement in a jail ministry for fifteen years at the Brevard County Jail in Sharpes, Florida, and my communication with people on social media convince me that many Christians long for the explanations behind their faith that will make it real to them. Additionally, whether young or old, inside the church or not, people want a better understanding of who they are and where they're going. People can't get away from their deep rooted desire to make sense of the huge amount of information, various relationships, and innumerable opportunities they face in life. They long to know how to fit the puzzle pieces of life together.

My experience also tells me that those who fail to see the big picture of God's plan tend to stumble the most. Truths offered in a piecemeal, disconnected fashion don't bring the clarity people yearn for. It's like trying to understand a car by viewing the parts before they're assembled. It's hard to imagine how all the pieces scattered on a garage floor can go 70 mph down the road.

The Beckoning

People within these groups, as well as many atheists, have asked me countless times to explain what combination of truths was so powerful that they convinced a staunch, atheist attorney to abandon everything he previously thought true. This book answers their questions. Along the way, I'll be sharing some of my life's experiences as well as how I processed the information I encountered on my journey from atheism to faith.

One of the numerous things I discovered was how God uses various "messengers" to beckon us to a relationship with Him. I'll be using these messengers to guide us through what I learned. Even though they work together, I'll describe them separately. That way, we can also investigate the part of the story each messenger tells.

As we go forward together, here's the path I plan to lead us on:

- In Chapters 2–9, we'll examine the messengers that God sends to beckon us to His truth. First, we'll investigate nature as God's creation, how His love for us is revealed in Scripture, and how Jesus represents the sum of all God's efforts to offer us His gift of great love. We'll then look at the unique way God uses our pain to draw us to Him. We'll also explore how God calls us to be a part of something greater than ourselves in the body of believers known as the Christian Church. Then, we'll take a look at how the consciousness God gave us serves to help us find Him and to love and serve others. And finally, we'll see how God uses His promise of an eternal life to help draw us to Him.

- In Chapter 10, we'll explore the counterfeiters—false messengers that attempt to blind us to what the true messengers are saying.
- In the final chapters, we'll see how God's messengers work and join together to voice His plan for our lives, proclaiming His unending love for us, and preparing us for our eternal home with Him.

As you travel with me on this incredible journey, like the astronauts who ventured to the moon and back, we'll strive to reach out and discover all we can. The reason is simple: If we don't seek, we won't find. Only by engaging our deepest curiosities do we possess a heart and mind truly open to the mysteries of God's truths.

Chapter 2

GOD'S MESSENGER: THE WORLD OF WONDER

"The heavens proclaim his righteousness, and all peoples see his glory."

PSALM 97:6

To view Michael's introductory video for Chapter 2, please go to www.michaelminot.com/thebeckoning

few years ago, I received a wake-up call while mountain biking and white water rafting with a friend in Canyonlands National Park. For months, I trained for the rigors of biking in a mountainous environment. So by the time my friend and I arrived in Utah, I felt ready to meet the physical demands of the trip. But within the first few moments of our trek across one of North America's most scenic landscapes, I quickly realized how emotionally unprepared I was for the awe-inspiring scenery. Breathless at times, I gazed out into what seemed to be surreal beauty—far more magnificent than brochures could possibly depict. Canyons carved by the slow motion of winding rivers drew my attention to one side, while towering red spires beckoned me on the other. When I looked up, occasionally I'd see an eagle drifting on the uplift generated from the canyon breezes. Mesmerized by the majestic views, many times I felt in danger of wrecking my bike as I tried to take in the scenery while negotiating the narrow paths along the sides of cliffs.

While I was caught off guard by this unexpected, overwhelming grandeur, what I observed after dousing the campfire each evening gave me even greater pleasure. With all traces of the sun absent from the sky, a brilliant panoramic show overhead replaced the landscape I admired below. During the darkest period of the moon's cycle in the darkest place in the continental United States, brilliant stars, more dazzling than any planetarium show, held me spell-bound. Appearing brighter than I had ever witnessed, the stars seemed so close, as if they were drawing me into their midst. I felt that I could almost, but not quite, reach out and touch the sky.

This combination of stunning landscapes and dazzling stars gave me a sense of being renewed, refreshed, and inspired.

Day after day and night after night, I struggled with my inability to comprehend the detail and magnificence of what I was witnessing. Prior to this trip, I had traveled to some of the largest and most culturally significant cities in the world. Also, I had visited many of the most prestigious museums that showcased some of mankind's finest creations and greatest achievements. But nothing in those cities or museums remotely compared to the natural wonders I witnessed in creation.

Seeing the nighttime heavens in this way helped me recognize how rarely I took the time to observe the world around me. The experience caused me to see what I'd been missing on so many star-filled nights throughout the years. And finally, the brilliance of the stars reminded me of what I discovered a few years earlier. During my personal investigation I learned how astronomers were discovering a complexity and design in the cosmos that staggers the imagination.

With these thoughts in mind, here are some of the more astonishing features in nature I came across during my personal investigation. Let's start by examining what the stars and planets reveal about their origin.

The Incredible Cosmos

A few hundred years ago, astronomers speculated that the heavens contained a few thousand stars. Even as recently as the early part of the twentieth century, astronomers didn't realize that the universe extends beyond our own galaxy.

Scientists now explore the far reaches of the universe, gazing through high-powered land-based and orbital telescopes. From these new instruments we know that the cosmos holds what scientists of the past never imagined: more than a billion galaxies! And within this cosmic cathedral, the smallest galaxies include fewer than a billion stars, while the largest contain more than a trillion.[2] Inside this unfathomably large universe lies our little neck of the woods, which centers on one of the more than two hundred billion stars in the Milky Way Galaxy.[3] To provide prospective, if a sphere 30 miles wide represented the size of the universe, our galaxy would approximate the top of a coffee cup.[4] And a small pencil point within that space represents our solar system—our sun and neighboring planets.

Remember learning in science class how the planets in our solar system revolve around the sun? What those Styrofoam and hanger models failed to show was the sun's immense size relative to the planets.

Few people realize the sun constitutes more than 99 percent of the solar system's entire composition.[5] In other words, within a scaled model of the solar system, if the sun were the size of a basketball, the earth would be the size of a pinhead.

This comparison helps us realize the exceptionally small size our planet holds relative to the cosmos. Within the entirety of the universe, the earth would seem nearly invisible and insignificant. But as we'll see, our earth maintains the perfect size in the most superb location to accomplish God's purposes. God meticulously designed an excellent place for us to live. In addition to its aesthetic beauty, the earth meets all our life-sustaining needs.[6]

The Precision of Our Solar System

While studying the features of the cosmos, I learned how Sir Isaac Newton—perhaps one of the brightest minds ever—was the first to observe the planets in sufficient detail to calculate their curving paths around the sun. Peering through his newly invented reflecting telescope in the late 1600s, he calculated with unprecedented accuracy the degree of gravitational influence the sun and each of the planets exert on each other considering their size, velocity, and distance from one another. He then observed how each of the eight planets maintains the exact size and speed necessary within this network to hold their courses. The degree of influence each of the planets exert on each other is just the right amount so that they all maintain their perpetual orbits around the sun.

Take the earth for example. It moves at a constant 67,000 mph. This precise speed, along with its size and distance to the sun all perfectly match the measurements necessary for the earth to maintain its perpetual orbit around the sun. If the earth traveled slower, it would be drawn into, and eventually collide with the sun. If it traveled any faster, the earth's velocity would propel it out of the solar system. But as Newton first noticed, the earth and the other planets maintain their separate and perfectly calibrated rates of speed.

Expressing his astonishment at these discoveries, Newton proclaimed, "This most beautiful system of the sun and planets could only proceed from the counsel and dominion of an Intelligent Being."[7]

As improbable as Newton believed this cosmic arrangement to be, he wasn't able to see the full complexity of our solar system. His telescope wasn't powerful enough to detect how the planets represent only a small portion of the entire arrangement. Imagine how astounded today's astronomers must be to find that more than 160 moons circle the planets and each participates in this same synchronized arrangement.[8]

Our Wonderful World and Its Partners

Recent research reflects how perfectly suited the sun and moon are to support life on earth. Our sun, for example, maintains the standing as one of the most stable stars ever observed. The sun's lack of volatility can be attributed in part to its unique location within the galaxy. Safely secluded away from the activity of other stars, the sun holds an unusually quiet spot between two spiral arms.

Without the gravitational interference or additional light from other stars, the sun's unique placement permits it to perform numerous functions critical to sustaining life on earth. The sun's uniform light output, varying just 0.1 percent, permits the earth to enjoy a stable climate. This consistency, as well as the rare and specific type of light emitted, makes photosynthesis possible.

Astronomers have also discovered how clusters of stars rotate around a central core area of our galaxy like blades on a fan. This is why our Milky Way is known as a spiral galaxy. They've also determined that a star within this type of galaxy located outside the spiral arms must maintain a specific distance from the core area to rotate at the same rate as the stars located in the spiral arms. Amazingly, our sun happens to be located at this exact distance. This precise placement then allows the sun to maintain its stable position. If the goal was to locate a star to support life—as it appears it was—our sun couldn't be more ideally situated.[9]

A Mountaintop Experience

Astronomers have found other reasons why our position in the galaxy is important. First, if our sun ever ventured closer to neighboring stars, light emanating from those stellar bodies could interfere with our climate. Light from sources other than our sun could also obscure our ability to see anything outside our atmosphere. In fact, light from other stars might prevent us from knowing that we live in a galaxy at all. Instead, we find our place in the galaxy free from other stars that could disturb our climate and prevent our view of the cosmos. As if on a mountain peak, we occupy the best seat imaginable to view and enjoy the splendors of the universe. Without being hindered by light from other stars, people everywhere have the privilege of observing what the heavenly bodies reveal about their creation. Impeccably situated for our needs, the earth's position in the universe is exquisitely stable, calm, and dark.

The Scriptures claim that none of these conditions occurred by accident. God gave these privileges to all people, no matter where they live, to fulfill one of His promises:

> The heavens declare the glory of God;
> the skies proclaim the work of his hands.
> Day after day they pour forth speech;
> night after night they reveal knowledge.
> They have no speech, they use no words;
> no sound is heard from them.
> Yet their voice goes out into all the earth,
> their words to the ends of the world.
>
> (PSALM 19:1–4)

Thus, God purposefully positioned the earth to allow its inhabitants to see the glories of His creation.

The Supernatural Fingerprint

I also learned from my investigation how astronomers have determined that the earth's distance from the sun perfectly matches what's necessary to maintain a life-sustaining environment. If the earth were even a fraction closer or farther away, life on our planet wouldn't be possible. Considering the proximity the earth holds to the sun, the earth spins once every day to provide just the right amount of warming and cooling the earth's surface needs.[10] Likewise, our planet's rotation around the sun generates the seasons. Each of these conditions fits perfectly with what we need.

Although few may think of the moon this way, it too plays a vital role in sustaining life on earth. Without its ideal size and position, the earth's tilt would vary widely causing severe climate shifts and extreme weather. The earth's tilt holds constant due to the moon's perfect size, distance, and rate of orbit. Without the moon's influence, the earth's exposure to the sun would become unpredictable and chaotic.[11]

Another fascinating aspect of the moon is how lunar gravity creates a slight bulge of water in its direction, as well as on the opposite side of the earth. As these surface water swells move across the globe, they generate the rise and fall of our ocean tides. This tidal action nourishes and cleanses the beaches and estuaries, creating habitat for many forms of life.[12]

These factors represent only a sampling of the wondrous perfections I found. There's not enough space for me to do anything other than allude to some of the other physical conditions making life on earth possible such as how the ozone layer protects us; the perfect fit that exists between the thickness of the earth's crust and the earth's seismic activity; as well as the amazingly fine-tuned proportions of oxygen to nitrogen and carbon dioxide to water vapor in the atmosphere. And what about how the earth generates its own magnetic shield to protect us from the lethal particles in the solar wind?

More and more, scientists are discovering that the earth and its cast of supporting partners form an extremely precise and complex planetary system. As mankind's discoveries have increased in the last few decades, we see with greater clarity how each part of the natural order proves to be well made for its purpose. Mounting scientific evidence makes it increasingly difficult to refuse to see how the many objects in our solar system all fit together to achieve the goals of an ingenious Creator. His fingerprints are clearly visible!

The Story of Life

While many scientists have devoted their lives to studying the cosmos, still others concentrate on the structures and habits of living beings. I found in my searching that although the questions arising from the material universe are complex, surpassing them is the fascinating aspect of life itself. How did life come to be? Where did plants and animals come from? How do these interdependent species exist alongside each other in a way that provides for their ongoing survival?

Long ago, scientists discovered how cells were the structural and functional units of all living organisms. They served as the information managers used to carry out life's functions. Today, we know much more about these microscopic wonders. Modern technology provides research scientists with the ability to study the details of cells at the atomic level. Just as super-sized telescopes have opened the cosmos to exploration, micron microscopes are unlocking the world within the cell. The result is an explosion of astounding new findings.

Some of the most recent discoveries reflect the enormous quantity of information contained within each human cell. Computer programmers provide instruction to computers utilizing sequences of ones and zeros like this: 100110100011. In a similar way, cells carry out their functions and know how to interrelate with other cells through instructions provided by the sequencing of four chemicals that scientists abbreviate as A, T, G, and C. The precise sequencing of these chemicals in human cells is referred to as DNA. The sequence of these four chemicals—which looks like TCCAGCACCG and so on—contains approximately 3.1 billion letters in every human cell. To put this into perspective, reading these letters in order at an average pace would take 31 years.[13]

Today, volumes of research data reveal the remarkable level of detail existing in the world of each cell. Prior to the recent burst of new information scientists never imagined:

- how cells take in and convert nutrients into energy;
- how cells employ encoded information;
- the molecular basis for inheritance;
- how cells use integrated circuits backed up by other circuits;
- the chemical process responsible for cell division.

The meticulous organization within each cell, distinct activity patterns, and precise chemical composition of cells prove to be astounding. No team of human architects could dream in such efficient and complex terms.[14]

The Marvelous Dance of Life

Specialized cells referred to as "eggs," represent the potential to produce a whole new living being. A separately identifiable life begins at the magical moment of fertilization. In an instant, a tiny egg cell becomes fused with the colossal amount of information necessary to multiply and grow into a mature being. Shortly after fertilization, the cell performs the amazing task of copying itself many times over. Within this division process, cells begin to take on special functions, assembling themselves into the various parts of a fully developed being.

Eventually, these cells will make up the highly ordered circulatory, digestive, reproductive, nervous, respiratory, and other organ systems. Though each organ group is a specialist of sorts, they all work together, coordinating their functions with one another.

So how many of these integrated functions take place at any one moment? An adult human, for example, maintains more than fifty trillion cells.[15] Each cell makes vital contributions to the specific organ it belongs to. Each system then constitutes but one of the many essential parts of a living being. And without all these myriad of coordinated cell functions, complex life would not be possible.

Perhaps even more astounding, mature cell groups form hundreds of different mammal and reptile species. Birds outnumber both of these combined. And the numbers of sea creatures are more numerous than birds. The different kinds of insects, butterflies, and beetles number in the tens of thousands. Untold numbers of microorganisms such as bacteria, fungi, and algae live in any moist area, including deep within the earth's crust.

Throughout it all, each species exhibits great diversity in size, shape, habitat, means of procreation, and many other qualities. The Scriptures claim that all this exists because God, as the Giver of life, purposed each being to play its unique role in the overall composition of life. Each creature sings its part in the harmony of nature's never finished song.

Life's Unlearned Behavior

Within this rich tapestry of life, I also found that each species carries a disposition toward certain unlearned behavior. Somehow, numerous varieties of birds are supplied with the knowledge of how to fly in the direction of the equator on the eve of winter and return home in the spring. Many birds fly thousands of miles during their semiannual migrations. Some navigate large bodies of water on their way to the same specific area year after year. Which one of us could do the same?

Young salmon hatchlings instinctively swim through unfamiliar waters from the only freshwater pool they know to the saltwater ocean. Years later, they carry out their perfectly timed return. How do they navigate hundreds of miles to the exact place of their birth? They act as if the calendar and a GPS device showed them the time and way.

Despite having a minimal capacity for understanding, honeybees and baby sea turtles also maintain a predisposition toward particular behaviors. To our amazement, honeybees know every aspect of the complex process necessary to build their perfect geometric combs. And immediately upon being hatched onto the beach, sea turtles display their unlearned behavior patterns by moving toward the water.

In fact, the more I investigated the behavior of all living beings, the more I found that each animal acts in certain ways not based on prior experience. By possessing these implanted behavior patterns, each species appears to carry out an intentionally given purpose supplied by the One who gave them life.

Somehow, it all holds together: the seasons brought about by the orbit and rotation of the earth, the food chain, and reproductive cycles. All of the parts appear as if they were designed to provide for each other in a way that perpetuates the great cycle of life. Similar to the cosmos, the Scriptures tell us that the complexity of the animal kingdom and its habitats were arraigned to invite us to see how God's fingerprints are embedded there too: "Ask the animals, and they will teach you, or the birds of the sky, and they will tell you, or speak to the earth, and it will teach you, or let the fish of the sea inform you." (Job 12:7-8)

The Human Ingredient

Investigating matters of science eventually led me to ponder the significance of my own existence as a human. After doing this, my degree of wonder multiplied many times over. Within the entire kingdom of living beings, I found that nothing compares to the complexity and magnificence of human life.

I began by taking an inventory of the characteristics I knew about myself. In a way that's beyond my comprehension, I grew from a single cell to the man I am today. I move, hear, think, feel, taste, and see in color. My body can also heal and reproduce. I remember details, dream dreams, gain knowledge, and experience feelings and emotions.

Scientists tell us that although they continue to make new discoveries, the biological complexity of the human body defies complete understanding. How our amazing mind works and interrelates with our body remains even further outside the realm of scientific understanding.

No other creature compares to us for yet another reason. Within our being, we harbor both the ability and the need to personally investigate what nature is trying to communicate to us. Animals know nothing of the complexities of the universe or their Maker. But we humans are equipped with every means necessary to contemplate the vast significance of all we see. We even possess the ability to anticipate the possibilities of what remains unseen.

My Findings

After sifting through all this information, some of the questions I ended up posing to myself were, "How likely was it that any one of these conditions I was learning about, much less all of them, could've appeared without help?" and "Was it more likely that these conditions were deliberately constructed or were they the results of random events?"

Though difficult at times and taking quite a while to get there, I eventually arrived at a number of conclusions. First, I recognized, statistically speaking, that no chance exists for each of these perfectly arranged circumstances to be a set of random coincidences. I found it difficult to believe that the hundreds of life-essential conditions found in nature could occur without intervention. The complexities of life and the intricate parts of the natural world work with an exactness that defies all odds. All systems—from the tiny cell to our place in the vast cosmos—operate with incredible precision. Nothing engineered by mankind remotely compares.

Next, I found that nature's awe-inspiring splendor seems to be designed to remind us of our innate need to question and determine how our life and the world we live in came to be. Simply by living in this elaborate world filled with such infinite beauty and detail, we cannot avoid the challenge of recognizing the Creator and appreciating the depth of His wisdom. As the Scripture says:

> "For since the creation of the world God's invisible qualities—His eternal power and divine nature—have been clearly seen, being understood from what has been made, so that men are without excuse."
>
> (ROMANS 1:20)

Taking up that challenge I found that nature's unbelievable specificity reveals a Creator with an incredible amount of intentionality, intelligence, and purpose. Though master artists have painted the beauty found in the natural world on canvas, I now see how the artistry of nature itself reigns supreme. Like a masterful composition, I recognize how God uses the harmony He placed within the interconnected parts of creation to display some of His most magnificent workmanship.

As one of His calling cards, the Creator supplies us with this never-ending yet always-changing face of nature. Fashioned like fine works of art, God blends beautiful combinations of shape, texture, and color into creation's intricate features. As an expression of His character, God specially made the incomprehensible grandeur, variety, and abundance of creation to excite our attention and point to the truth of our origin.

I've also come to realize that God made us to be attracted to the scenery in the great outdoors. Gazing upon the sea as the sun touches the water brings us a sense of calm. Whistles from songbirds welcoming a new day relax us. We pause in awestruck amazement at the sight of majestic snow-covered mountains. Intricate color patterns displayed on flowers and tropical fish astound us. Amazement fills us as we take in the fragrance of a rose or ponder how rainbows paint colors across the sky.

When we pause to contemplate the environment around us, something within the depth of our beings appreciates its beauty. The majestic manner that nature uses to display itself lifts our hearts and refreshes our minds.

Considering all this, I've often wondered since becoming a believer what kind of God would make all these things for our benefit? What admiration and gratitude is appropriate to a Creator like that?

The Beckoning

By rushing here and there, we can easily miss the truths communicated by the wonders around us. When we don't savor these natural gifts, we betray our inherent need to connect with this vital source of truth. Instead, as seekers of truth, we must take time away from life's expressway to admire God's magnificent works and consider the infinite wisdom it reflects. We should follow those who go out at midnight to consider the work of God's fingers in the stars. By doing so, we allow creation to exert its power to awaken our childhood curiosity.

For other creatures, nature is simply their living environment. But for us, these wonderful surroundings embody so much more. Nature represents a chorus of sights, sounds, and aromas that summon us to recognize its grandeur and magnificence. No matter the angle of our view, the natural order beckons us to see what the Creator has made.

Even the word *nature* sounds like sweet music to us. With God as the conductor, the physical features of the universe seem to rejoice in their freedom to sing the harmonies of creation's song. Each lends its voice to singing the divine universal anthem for all to hear.

In the course of nature's choreographed performance, God issues His ongoing invitation for each of us to join the music and draw near to Him. Indeed, some who have taken the time to truly listen now dance to the music with endless joy.

Think It Through! Talk It Over!

1. What natural wonder has caused you to wonder how it came into existence? To what, if anything, did you attribute its origin?

2. How did you reach that conclusion?

3. How does the detailed order in the natural world cause you to consider the possibility that God made everything?

4. Why do you agree or disagree that the vast diversity of living things points to a Creator rather than evolution?

5. How is our planet's position in the universe perfect for the sustaining of human life? What thoughts does this phenomenon bring to mind?

6. Do you believe more people would recognize the Creator's fingerprints in nature if they would slow their pace of living? Why or why not?

7. Why do you believe the theory of evolution appeals to those who subscribe to it?

8. Why do you agree or disagree that it takes faith to believe in the theory of evolution?

9. Would you agree that it takes more faith to believe in evolution than in creation? Explain your answer.

10. What thoughts come to mind when you gaze into a starry sky?

GOD'S MESSENGER: THE SCRIPTURES

"For the word of God is alive and active. Sharper than any double-edged sword, it penetrates even to dividing soul and spirit, joints and marrow; it judges the thoughts and attitudes of the heart."

HEBREWS 4:12

To view Michael's introductory video for Chapter 3, please go to www.michaelminot.com/thebeckoning

ometimes simple incidents can leave lasting impressions. One evening, during my first few months as a voluntary chaplain at the Brevard County Jail in Florida, a guard was escorting me to my assigned classroom. Along the way, I recognized a prisoner being escorted by another guard on the other side of the hallway. "Hey, Andrew!" I called out.

Raising his head and mustering a half smile as he continued to hobble forward in his shackles and handcuffs, Andrew responded, "Hey, Mike!"

"Hope you're okay… considering," I replied.

Continuing to shuffle along with his escort beside him, he shrugged, "You know how it goes in here, Mike. I'm just doin' my time, man; just doin' my time."

"Take care," I said. "You too," Andrew responded.

Other than the coincidence of bumping into someone I hadn't seen in years, I thought little of the incident at the time. Over the following months, however, I came to realize how Andrew's attitude represented one of two primary coping techniques I observed inmates use while adjusting to life in jail. Andrew represented those who purposefully sink themselves into a dreamlike fog taking on zombie-like characteristics. Thinking about the choices that brought them to this place in life is too painful. Sadly, my weekly experiences at the jail revealed to me that those who adopt a "just doin' my time" strategy often leave prison the same way they entered: harboring a mass of pent-up anger, confusion, and bitterness.

Others adopt a different, more fitting strategy—one that offers much greater potential. During the early weeks of confinement many inmates go through an intense time of soul searching. With the normal course of their daily lives severely disrupted and lots of time on their hands, they wonder what's happened to their lives.

During my visits to the jail, I tried to seize on what the inmates were going through. Though nobody relishes incarceration, I challenged the inmates to realize that their time in jail could provide an ideal opportunity to consider what changes they might want to make in their lives. I began by saying, "No one's required to leave jail the same way they came in. Neither the walls of the jail nor the shackles you wear to court can bind you as securely as your attitude about life." I told them how I'd witnessed the attitudes of some inmates change so dramatically that it almost seemed appropriate to give them new names when they walked out the jail's front door. That's how much their outlook changed about themselves, about other people, and about life generally.

Taking a page from my own life's history, I sometimes described the critical time when I reevaluated my life and studied the Scriptures for the first time. I'd begin by telling the inmates how for many years I'd kept my heart and mind in a concrete vault. I determined that no one could tell me what to think or how to live my life. True to the stubborn attitude I held, when I finally arrived at the point of investigating what the Scriptures said, I was determined to come to my own conclusions. No one was going to talk me into anything. Most evenings I poured over the passages while lying on my couch at home alone. I didn't want help from anyone.

Strangely, during my first couple weeks of reading, I developed a curiosity for how many of the passages described historical events I'd studied in history class. Some of the poetry was also intriguing. But after a couple months of studying, I was shocked at what started to happen. I began to suspect I was examining something far more significant than simply well written ancient literature. As I continued reading, the details of why the people, creatures, and things around me exist began to unfold before me.

The more I searched the Scriptures and the scientific evidences of our origin, the more I sensed something deep within me beginning to change. I found it increasingly difficult to dismiss what I was reading in the Scriptures as fairytales. At some point I started to equate my eager reading of the Scriptures to a thirsty desert wanderer who just found an oasis bubbling with fresh water.

In the end, my investigation convinced me that what I once so arrogantly condemned as utter foolishness was, in fact, the truth. I came to view the Bible as a loving invitation from our Creator to investigate all He'd planned for those who are willing to accept His gracious love. More than a book on how to improve everyday living, the Bible serves as a guide to our future by telling us where we came from and why we are here.

After inviting the inmates to consider my story, I challenged them to avoid the "just doin' time" attitude and instead seize the opportunity to invest their abundant free time searching for answers to the deep questions they harbored about life and about themselves by reading the Bible.

Over the years, a large number of inmates took up my challenge. Many of the free Bibles issued by the chaplain's office showed up in my class in the hands of eager learners with their covers falling off and pages soiled from constant use. When I asked the group to open their Bibles to a particular passage, many knew the words of the passage by heart. When I paused during my teaching to encourage input, many offered related Scripture passages for consideration. It was easy to see who had discovered and cherished the truths in the Bible.

Now, let's focus our attention more directly on what makes the Scriptures stand apart from all literature. We know from our investigation in the previous chapter that nature points us *toward* God. But what we're about to see is that the Scriptures are a trustworthy source of truth *about* Him.

Discovered Treasure

The words in the Bible began to be penned nearly 3,500 years ago. As I first read the Scriptures, it was interesting to me how dozens of writers spanning 1,400 to 1,500 years created this collective work. A great many of them played the role of historian while others composed poetry with wonderful skill. Some held positions of great nobility with a few carrying the title of king. Others were prophets; some just commoners.[16]

But what captivated me the most was what the Scriptures say. Let's start with the big picture view.

Essentially, the Scriptures claim that the universe had a beginning. Within the vastness of the cosmos God created, He took great pains to create an elaborate stage for man to live. As we saw in the previous chapter, God made the earth, sun, moon, and stars, followed by the plants and animals. Then, God meticulously made human beings in His image placing many attributes of His divine nature in them. These details, so the Scriptures say, were all part of God's original plan to give us everything we needed so we could enjoy perfect intimacy with Him forever. But as we surely know, our condition today doesn't reflect this intimacy. Something dreadful happened.

Soon after man was placed in the marvelous setting created for him, the Scriptures go on to claim that our first parents, Adam and Eve, abandoned living life God's way. By choice, they disconnected themselves from the source of what made them good and by doing this exposed all their descendants to untold destructive passions. Since then, as history demonstrates, our rebellious attitudes have carried us far from our original nature.

Considering the level of disappointment God must have experienced, He could've walked away leaving man to fend for himself. Or, He could've destroyed everything and started over. But if God had chosen either of these options, the central theme of the Scriptures, which is God's unfailing love for us, wouldn't be true. Fortunately, instead of choosing either of these options, God crafted a plan to bring about our restored relationship with Him. But carrying out this plan wouldn't be easy.

The cornerstone of God's efforts focused on Jesus, God's Son, and His willingness to carry out two primary tasks. First, Jesus would become human so He could teach us in the most direct way possible how much God loves us and that He created us to love Him in return. Then, in what would mark the pivotal point of all history, as the ultimate demonstration of God's love, Jesus would offer Himself as a living sacrifice in order to overcome all the sins of mankind.

God revealed some of the more astonishing parts of this plan long before it was carried out. He told Isaiah how Jesus would be "despised and rejected by men, a man of sorrows, and familiar with suffering." (Isaiah 53:3). As a result, Jesus would endure great pain during His human life. Some of those He came to save would end up torturing Him causing "his appearance to become disfigured beyond that of any man and his form marred beyond human likeness." (52:14). But despite the atrocity and unfairness of it all, "He wouldn't open his mouth; he would be led like a lamb to the slaughter, as a sheep before her shearers is silent, so he would not open his mouth." In the end, however, after He was "pierced for our transgressions" (53:5), "he would be raised and lifted high." (52:13).

Nice story! But was it true? Many, like me, tend to doubt what they can't see and touch. So, what began to captivate me, even beyond the story itself, was how it appeared that God knew we would need help believing the full depth of what He tells us in the Scriptures. I came to learn how He uses several means to authenticate the Scriptures as His divinely inspired words. Let's take a look at how the Bible provides us these important measures of reliability.

God's Authenticating Process

First, more than any other religious book, the Bible mentions specific people and the places where they lived. The Scriptures often used events that deeply impacted these ancient cultures to serve as the backdrop for its teaching about spiritual matters. Therefore, one way to test the Scriptures is to determine whether the many people and places mentioned in the Bible actually existed, or were they characters and settings in a fictional story.

One of the thoughts that crossed my mind when I began reading the Scriptures was how so many of the physical features mentioned were subjects I'd studied in junior high geography class. I later learned how scholars have concluded that the mountains, rivers, lakes, and valleys referred to in the Bible match the landscape we see today. Further, many of the cities have maintained not only the same location since biblical times, but also their names. I've personally had the privilege of being baptized in the Jordan River, swimming in the Dead Sea, taking a boat ride on the Sea of Galilee, and standing on both Mount Zion and the Mount of Olives. I've also had the opportunity of walking through the streets of such ancient biblical cities as Jerusalem, Bethlehem, and Capernaum, to name a few. Since biblical times, each generation has passed on these names to the next, thereby preserving them to the current day—some for more than 3,000 years.

Many scholars have also determined that the people groups and their leaders mentioned in the Bible correspond to the historical records from that era. To my surprise, of the untold number of statements about people or places in the Bible, no contradictions have been found with any other historical source. From ancient writings; to the ruins of palaces, government buildings, amphitheaters, and tombs; to the pottery, coins, art, and other remnants of civilizations; the details of the Bible continue to be verified.

Because of the wealth of confirming archaeological evidence that continues to pour in, skeptics are finding that their list of objections has decreased dramatically year-by-year. Prior to the 1900s, skeptics claimed a number of ancient people groups and kings mentioned in the Scriptures never existed because they were unknown outside the biblical record. For example, Belshazzar was mentioned as a King of Babylon in Daniel 5. But, the last known King of Babylon was Nabonidus. Without any evidence outside the Scriptures, secular scholars also dismissed the entire Hittite Empire as fictional. For the same reason, they claimed the Assyrian king named Sargon mentioned in Isaiah 20 never lived.

But the archaeological movement born in the early part of the last century has produced an overwhelming amount of evidence that overcomes many of these assertions. By virtue of the enhanced ability to travel, new technologies, and funding from both governmental and private sources, expeditions in the Middle East began discovering ancient ruins and artifacts at an unprecedented rate. By the end of the twentieth century, tens of thousands of factual assertions made in the Bible had been confirmed by independent, non-religious sources. Specific examples include the clay tablets that were recently discovered near modern-day Bagdad confirming Belshazzar as Nabonidus' son who served as co-regent with his father.[17] Clay tablets discovered in Turkey mark the location that once served as the Hittite capital.[18] And Sargon's palace was discovered in Iraq.[19]

The more I read about these matters, the more difficulty I experienced comprehending this over-abundance of compelling evidence favoring the conclusion that the Scriptures are trustworthy. I also learned that because of this overwhelming evidence, many in the secular archaeology community have made an about face. Unlike those of one hundred years ago, a great number of today's scholars not only respect the Scriptures for its historical accuracy but also use them as a primary research tool. Many suggest that no other ancient manuscript, secular or religious, contains the level of proven detail contained in the Scriptures.

God's Authenticating Process: The Prophecies

I also learned from my research how the Bible could be tested in another manner. Comprising almost one fourth of Scripture,[20] the Bible contains more than 1,000 detailed prophecies—approximately 800 in the Old Testament and 200 in the New Testament. By their sheer numbers as well as the supernatural nature of what they do, the prophecies force us to ask "Who except God could accurately forecast hundreds of events in advance and then bring them to pass?" [21] Let me summarize a few examples to show you what my investigation was uncovering.

Most of the prophecies I found were recorded after God gave direct revelation of the future to one individual. Several examples fit into that category. First, God gave Daniel incredible details of the future fate of the Greek empire. As if writing about something he just observed, in the 6th century BC Daniel described with perfection the Empire's future division into four parts and how two of the parts would remain in conflict over the land of Israel (Daniel 11:1-19).

History tells us that three centuries later, from 336 to 323 BC, Alexander the Great reigned as the mighty king of the Greek Empire. As a result of Alexander's many military victories, including his conquest over the vast domain held by the Persians, the empire experienced an unprecedented expansion of power. But at what seemed the pinnacle of Greek supremacy, Alexander died at age 32. His death set off a tumultuous internal battle for power amongst other would-be kings. But the fierce struggle for succession never resulted in a new king. Rather, just as Daniel predicted, the Greek Empire met its demise and was divided into the four lesser kingdoms of Greece, Asia Minor, Syria, and Egypt. [22]

Another prediction was recorded by Isaiah 150 years in advance of an actual event which described how the Babylonians would be conquered by people referred to as the Medes. At the time of this prediction around 700 BC, Babylon was a mighty nation with advanced technology well beyond any of its rivals including that of the Medes. Vindicating Isaiah against those who laughed and scoffed at such an unlikely scenario, the Medes later attacked and prevailed over the Babylonians.

Around 600 BC, Jeremiah predicted that the Babylonians would conquer the Israelite tribes of Judah and Benjamin. As part of his prediction, he indicated the Jews would also endure seventy years of captivity after being conquered. History shows how these events occurred in the 4th and 5th centuries BC (Jeremiah 25:9-13).

A second type of prophecy I found provides more than one hundred descriptions of events or circumstances to occur in the life of the Messiah, the person God promised to send to save and restore Israel. Careful reading of these passages reveals Jesus to be the one who fulfilled each of these prophecies. We'll take a closer look at many of these prophecies when we examine the life of Jesus in the next two chapters.

It was interesting to me how none of the passages I read in the Gospels included an explanation from Jesus as to how an event in His life fulfilled one of the prophecies. And without exception, not until after Jesus' death, did His disciples begin to understand how the events of Jesus' life matched so perfectly with what the prophets predicted. Only following Jesus' resurrection and reappearance did His followers make the connections between the messianic prophecies and what occurred during Jesus' life. It's hard to fault them for their oversight, however. Today, almost 2,000 Easters later, a great number of people continue to struggle with the precision with which all these prophecies were carried out.

Prior to my investigation I'd never paid any attention to the prophecies in Scripture much less considered their impact. But by the end of my studies they posed one of the greatest challenges to my thinking. I was forced to admit that the extraordinary accuracy and detail of hundreds of prophecies didn't leave me or anyone else who challenge the Scriptures much wiggle room. Regardless, I read numerous accounts of critics who continued to hold to their position. Though forced to acknowledge how most of the prophecies have been fulfilled and none proven inaccurate, many skeptics take the position that some of the prophecies are *too* accurate.

Take the prophecy of Daniel for example. Some skeptics argue that no one could predict with such flawless accuracy how the Greek Empire would breakup into four specific parts and how two of them would remain in conflict. Accordingly, they suggest Daniel either lived during the time the events took place or later. In other words, he couldn't have lived before the events took place. By asserting this unsupported claim, however, these doubters inadvertently highlighted to me how no *unassisted* human could foresee the future in such startling detail.

Whether describing future conflicts and their outcomes, predicting the details of the coming Messiah, or giving an account of other events, my research into the prophecies provided me strong indications that I could trust the words of the Bible. By recording such a large number of exceptionally specific predictions and insuring they came to pass, God provided an important measure of reliability for the accuracy of the Scriptures. I ended up posing the same question that Augustine asks, "What can be more trustworthy than that which narrates past events and predicts the future with equal clearness...?" [23]

Miracles

By the time I finished my investigation, I also came to realize how the claim that many miracles have occurred furnish yet another compelling source of evidence for the accuracy of the Scriptures. The position I held when starting my studies was that miracles aren't possible. Skeptics believe the laws of nature are unchangeable and always perform in certain predictable ways.[24] The only acceptable proof of what's real, I would have said, is what can be demonstrated and reproduced in the laboratory. Consequently, skeptics dismiss all of what the Scriptures say, from the beginning to the end, claiming the accounts of these "inconceivable events" taint the entire work.

Like so many others, I refused to consider what couldn't be seen through the lens of science. The underlying truth, however, was that I didn't want miracles to be possible. I knew that if the laws of nature could be bent, that would require a Bender.

As I studied the relevant passages I began to realize that most of the hundreds of documented miracles were claimed to be observed by many people. For example, the Bible describes how a man's walking stick changed into a snake before many witnesses (Exodus 7:10-12). Later, possibly thousands of others witnessed that same stick budding a flower (Numbers 17:1-5). In a different time and place, with many inhabitants inside, the walls of a fortressed city fell flat when the attacking army merely gave a great shout (Joshua 2:1-11). On another occasion, after one man died from the heat while standing too close to a fiery pit, three other men, to the amazement of many onlookers, emerged from the middle of the pit unsinged (Daniel 3:19-27).

Some of the more recent miracles documented in Scripture were alleged to have been performed by Jesus—thirty-seven recorded in all. But these may just be a sample of the full number He actually performed. The closing verse of John's Gospel says, "Jesus did many other things as well. If every one of them were written down, I suppose that even the whole world would not have room for the books that would be written" (John 21:25).

My review of the biblical accounts of Jesus' miracles revealed that He almost always performed them in the midst of large crowds or that the results became known to many people. Here are three examples of the many that caught my attention. The first involves the account of the healing of a paralyzed man. The Scriptures claim that Jesus was teaching in one of the houses in Capernaum after returning from healing many people of their various sicknesses and diseases in the surrounding villages of Galilee. By this time, people from all over Galilee and Judea, including some Pharisees, had come to investigate reports of Jesus' healing powers. Four men carrying a paralyzed man on a stretcher attempted to reach Jesus. After being unable to reach Him because of the crowds, they carried the man upstairs to the roof of the house where Jesus was teaching and let him down through an opening in the roof. After Jesus healed the paralyzed man, the man stood up, picked up his bed and walked out of the house glorifying God. (See Mark 2.)

The second story involves the Jewish leaders in Jerusalem. The Scriptures claim that Jesus healed a beggar who'd been blind from birth. Family, neighbors, and others, including the Pharisees, recognized him as the man who was previously blind. After being questioned by the Pharisees, the man confirmed that Jesus was responsible for giving him his sight. To make sure this was the man the Pharisees knew as the blind beggar, they also questioned his parents. (See John 9.)

The third story involves the death of Lazarus, a friend of Jesus who lived just outside Jerusalem in a community called Bethany. After Lazarus became ill, his sisters sent word to Jesus. However, by the time Jesus arrived, Lazarus had died and had been in a tomb for four days. Upon His arrival, Jesus greeted a crowd of mourners including Lazarus's sisters. Surprising everyone, He asked some of the mourners to remove the stone from the entrance to Lazarus' burial place. He faced the tomb, prayed to the Father, and shouted, "Lazarus, come out!" Immediately, Lazarus hobbled out of the tomb with his grave close wrapped around him. (See John 11.)

Though the claim that someone was raised from the dead is a remarkable assertion, from an evidentiary standpoint, what struck me most is how the story ended.

> "Therefore many of the Jews who came to visit Mary [one of Lazarus's sisters], and had seen what Jesus did, put their faith in him. But some of them went to the Pharisees and told them what Jesus had done. Then

the chief priests and the Pharisees called a meeting of
the Sanhedrin."

(JOHN 12:45-48)

To me, the fact the Scriptures indicated that the governing body of
Jewish leaders in Jerusalem were told what happened raises the credibility
of the story substantially. If Lazarus wasn't walking around for everyone
to see, I'd expect the Jewish leaders to vehemently deny that he rose
from the dead as soon as they first heard someone make that claim. But
I couldn't find any record of a denial.

My Point of Reckoning

Considering that I'm a lawyer, I felt somewhat embarrassed after reading
how the Scriptures described so many miracles occurring before so many
witnesses. Judges and attorneys tell jurors that they're to search for the
truth by analyzing the testimony of the witnesses and other evidence
presented at trial. If numerous witnesses testify to a certain matter
without any contradictory evidence being presented, a presumption of
correctness is applied because the testimony is undisputed. Somehow,
up to this point in my life, I failed to apply any similar standard or fair
method of judging the miracles documented in the Scriptures. To the
extent I paid any attention at all to the Scriptures, I didn't recognized the
number of witnesses claiming to have seen the miracles firsthand and
whether anyone else offered a different account.

By making the claim that thousands of people throughout history
witnessed hundreds of miracles, it appeared to me that the Scriptures
established yet another means of testing the Bible's credibility. If any
account of a miraculous event was false, we'd expect objections to be
waged by those living at the time the Scripture describing the miracle
was written. To this point, let's again focus on the Scriptures that claim
Jesus performed many miracles in the first century AD. Secular historians

of that time such as Josephus confirm Jesus' widespread notoriety throughout Palestine in the last years of his life. But none wrote about witnesses who contradicted the claims of those that described how Jesus performed many great miracles.

Instead, of all the eyewitnesses to these events, or even the circumstances that surrounded the event, I was unable to find the account of *anyone* who knew or heard of what happened who ever waged an objection to the scriptural account of these events. In other words, no record exists of witnesses who offered a different version of the story that challenged the claim that these miracles occurred.

I also discovered a couple other reasons why believers don't struggle to reach the conclusion that miracles are possible. Unlike skeptics, they view the situation quite differently. First, once someone agrees that the universe and all its inhabitants were created by God, the unbelievable amount of knowledge and power that must be held by this Creator causes all other miracles to look like small potatoes. Secondly, the amazing nature and proof authenticating the prophecies cause them to be one form of miracles.

Lastly, after pondering on these issues for some time, I came to the stark realization that it only takes one miracle. If I came to the conclusion that the fixed laws of nature have been broken even once, my worldview would be thrown into chaos. My belief that science and only science reveals what's true was being put to a severe test.

So, by the end of my investigation I had yet another issue to ponder. Are miracles possible? As you know, in the end, I determined that beyond what any man could do on his own, miracles are possible. And because they're possible, they reflect the intervention of a power not limited by human constraints. Every miracle, standing on its own, demonstrates how a Force above nature's laws interacts in our world. Like the prophecies, these public displays of supernatural power help substantiate the truth of the Bible and the "Who" behind it all.

Jesus Affirmed the Divine
Authorship and Authority of Scripture

During my reading of the Gospels, I discovered another reason some people believe in the Bible. The four Gospels record more than a dozen times how Jesus cited the Scriptures as the authority for His teaching. He mentioned many historical figures from the Scriptures such as Noah, Moses, Abraham, David, and Elisha. He also referred to events such as what occurred at Sodom and Gomorrah.

In his book *Loving God*, Charles Colson summarized Jesus' extensive use of Scripture.

"When He began His ministry, Christ used Scripture to announce His commission. 'The Spirit of the Lord is upon me, because he has anointed me to preach good news to the poor. He has sent me to proclaim freedom from the prisoners and recovery of sight to the blind, to release the oppressed, to proclaim the year of the Lord's favor.' He read from the scroll of Isaiah. Indeed He repeatedly cited the Old Testament Scriptures as the authority for His work and the verification of His person. He used the Word as His sole defense against Satan and He asked His Father to sanctify His disciples in the truth"[25]

C. S. Lewis commented on how Jesus connected Himself to the Scriptures this way:

"We are committed to the Hebrew Scriptures in principle by our Lord Himself. On that famous journey to Emmaus He found fault with the two disciples for not believing what the prophets had said. They ought to have known from their Bibles that the Anointed One, when He came, would enter his glory through suffering. He then explained, from "Moses" (the Pentateuch) down, all the places in the Old Testament "concerning Himself" (Luke 24:25-27). He clearly identified Himself with a figure often mentioned in the Scriptures; appropriated to himself many passages which a modern scholar might see no such reference."[26]

The Beckoning

When I first began reading the Scriptures, I found them difficult to understand. I read certain portions two or three times before moving on. Often, I couldn't get the pieces to fit. For awhile it didn't feel like I was accomplishing anything more than accumulating a lot of loose ends.

Though my initial lack of understanding frustrated me, I also found many of the passages intriguing. So, instead of getting drowsy or tired, I found myself not being able to go to bed. Although I needed rest for my next day's work, well into the night I pondered the significance of all I was reading. This process repeated itself night after night and weekend after weekend.

Eventually, however, there came a point when I began to grasp the historical context of the Bible, who the authors were and their various styles of writing. This helped me recognize how some of the individual passages could be part of a larger story. I also began to see how the spiritual lessons embedded in the stories could be part of a larger, over-all truth. There came a point when I almost couldn't take it all in. Although I found my mind racing, each page took an inordinate amount of time to read. There was so much to ponder that I was nearly overwhelmed. Never before had I read information with such incredible density.

Though confused at first, in the end, the story we're investigating in this book eventually unfolded before me. And what a story it is! Little did I know when I first started reading the Scriptures that I was sitting on a launch pad poised to take me on the most exciting journey of my life.

From these experiences I learned numerous lessons including why the Scriptures speak of itself in this way:

"For the word of God is alive and active. Sharper than any double-edged sword, it penetrates even to dividing soul and spirit, joints and marrow; it judges the thoughts and attitudes of the heart."

(HEBREWS 4:12)

I further learned how the principles described in the Scriptures don't change. In the legal profession, lawyers advocate their clients' positions by citing the applicable rules of law. Legal research is made more challenging, however, by the fact that legislative amendments and new court decisions continually modify the state of the law. The fluctuating nature of man's law requires attorneys to update their research continually. But unlike man's ever shifting rules and case law, the Scriptures remain unchanged throughout all generations. The apostle Peter observed, "All people are like grass, and all their glory is like the flowers of the field; the grass withers and the flowers fall, but the word of the Lord endures forever" (1 Peter 1:24-25).

I also came to realize how God gives us both the Bible and nature as two separate, yet compatible means through which He offers us truth. Both originate from the same Author with the same intent. Each complements the other. In different ways, each points to the same thing.

From the Scriptures, God also shows us how He sends us additional messengers. As we continue our investigation, they will be the subject of our inquiry in the next few chapters.

Think It Through! Talk It Over!

1. What is your opinion of the Bible? Why do you hold that opinion?

2. Why would you agree or disagree that forty different writers in different locations and writing at different times without any collaboration would be unable to write a book having a central theme and perfect unity?

3. In Isaiah 53, Isaiah wrote specifically about Jesus' death about 775 years before it occurred. What does that fact tell you about the Bible?

4. Numerous archaeological discoveries have confirmed the existence of many people and places mentioned in the Bible. How should you respond to this archaeological evidence?

5. According to John 20:30-31, what was the main purpose of Jesus' miracles? Has this purpose been fulfilled in your life? Why or why not?

6. What significance, if any, do you attach to the fact that so many Biblical prophecies have been fulfilled precisely?

7. Why do you think Jesus performed His miracles in public?

8. What excuses might keep some individuals from reading the Bible?

9. What attitude should a seeker of truth bring to his or her reading of the Bible?

10. How do you account for the fact that the Bible has endured for 2,000 years in spite of numerous attempts to discredit it or destroy?

Chapter 4

JESUS: GOD HIMSELF
AS MESSENGER

"The Word became flesh and made his dwelling among us. We have seen his glory, the glory of the one and only Son, who came from the Father, full of grace and truth."

JOHN 1:14

To view Michael's introductory video for Chapter 4, please go to www.michaelminot.com/thebeckoning

*D*uring the summer after my first year in law school, I had the privilege of studying in Oxford, England. In the midst of our seven-week program, three other students and I decided to take a weekend and explore Scotland. I had read about some of the touristy sites in Edinburgh. One of the others had heard about some interesting things we could see in Glasgow and the Highlands area. But with little more than that to go on, along with a map and a visitor's guide, we trekked off to the train station the next morning ready for whatever came our way.

After hours of viewing the beautiful, green countryside from our train, we arrived in Edinburgh late one Thursday evening. As we checked into our budget-oriented hostel, the front desk clerk asked if we had come to observe Princess Anne's royal review of the Scottish Guard the next morning. Surprised, I indicated we knew nothing about Princess Anne's visit. That night, we changed the tentative plans we had made on the train, and opted instead to view English tradition at its finest.

Early the next morning we staked out the best spot possible to view the spectacle. We were far from the first to arrive, however. Droves of people had come to see and welcome the princess. With banners attached to all the street light poles and extra-large signs on some of the buildings, the city looked all dressed up for the occasion.

Minutes before the parade began, the princess and her entourage entered the viewing station on the opposite side of the street from the crowds. Dressed exquisitely for the occasion in a beautiful yellow dress, the princess reviewed the parade as it marched down Princes Street. With the historic Castle of Edinburgh directly behind Princess Anne, waves of Scottish Guard units, along with drum and bagpipe groups, proudly marched by. Some of the soldiers wore formal military attire. Others donned fatigues. Regardless, every piece of metal was polished and shined. Every stitch of clothing was pressed to the standard of a strict military inspection.

Have you ever heard someone play the "pipes" in person? Loud, aren't they! Bagpipes can produce one of the highest decibel readings for a wind instrument. Can you imagine what *thirty* bagpipes followed by a line of base drums sounds like?

The crowds, and especially those in the parade, seemed to burst with all the pride of Scotland. I left Edinburgh only imagining what the grandeur of a royal wedding or coronation must be like.

Anyone acquainted with the long, rich history of the British Empire can understand the significance the people of Edinburgh placed on the princess's visit. But even the most casual visitor like me, having little understanding of British tradition, would have found it difficult to avoid being caught up in the precision and glamour of the celebration.

My Lack of Understanding

The manner in which I entered my investigation of the life of Jesus was not unlike my preparations before leaving for Scotland. Vaguely speaking, I was already aware of a number of the Christian claims concerning Jesus before I started; especially the stories behind Christmas and Easter. While in elementary school, I attended a number of plays portraying the circumstances surrounding the beginning or end of Jesus' life. In junior high I had occasion to read portions of the New Testament. As I became older, particularly during my college years, I was approached by Christians who wanted to explain their views of Christianity. From these experiences I understood that Jesus was the central figure of the New Testament. I knew that if I was to better understand the claims of Scripture, I needed to probe much deeper into the circumstances of Jesus' life.

I began with a flood of questions swirling in my head. I wondered why Jesus, the person the Scriptures claims is the world's Creator, would even consider transforming Himself into a human being. What was He up to? Why would such a thing be desirable or necessary? Why were God's other messengers insufficient to provide everything that humans needed? Could not the messengers of nature and the Scriptures suffice? Intuitively, the notion of God taking on human flesh seemed counterintuitive.

Because of the prominent place Jesus held in the Scriptures, my theory was that if I could get a good grip on what the Scriptures said about Him, my ability to understand the rest of Scripture would be greatly enhanced. So, I entered this part of my investigation with the attitude that I'd slow down, be extra methodical and willing to invest the necessary time to dig into the texts. Eventually, my investigation revealed a wealth of information I never imagined existed. I found the depth of the story behind the person of Jesus to be far more profound than I ever suspected. Through the remainder of this chapter and all of the next, I'll explain what I learned from my research of the Gospels and the rest of the New Testament.

Great Expectations

In a way similar to how the Scots held such great anticipation of the Princess Anne's visit, in the years immediately before Jesus' birth, many Jews expected that royalty would soon visit them. Some believed the time was near for the arrival of the great and powerful king spoken of in Scripture, the one representing all truth. In his book *Simply Christian*, N.T. Wright describes this expectation:

"Not all Jews of this period believed in or wanted a coming Messiah. But those who did, and they were many, cherished a frequently repeated set of expectations as to what the anointed one would do when he arrived. He would fight the battle against Israel's enemies—specifically, the Romans. He would rebuild, or at least cleanse and restore, the Temple. He would bring Israel's long history to its climax, reestablishing the monarchy as in the days of David and Solomon. He would be God's representative to Israel, and Israel's representative to God."[27]

Those who studied Old Testament prophecies believed the arrival of this Savior—the Messiah—would mark the dawn of irrevocable change in the world's social order and systems of government. They expected the Messiah to impose and enforce God's law. And how would this King of all kings announce His arrival? They expected He would present Himself to the world with the formality befitting the highest and mightiest earthly king, something far grander than what I observed in Scotland.

God Becomes Human

History reveals that the timing of these expectations was spot on. But many Jews living in the first century misinterpreted the prophesied descriptions of the Messiah, how He would arrive, and the purpose for His coming. As a result, they totally failed to recognize Him. Unlike what most Jewish leaders anticipated, the Gospels assert that the Messiah wasn't born into a family of great power. Additionally, He didn't come to seek high office or to conquer nations. Nor did He pursue riches. He also didn't come to raise one people over another or to start a new religion. Ironically, the Messiah was born in humble surroundings and subsequently led a simple life. Most surprisingly, the Gospels proclaim Him not merely as the last in a long line of prophets or another of God's representatives to Israel, but God incarnate.

Though the Messiah is referred to in Scripture as the "king of kings" (Ezekiel 26:7), Jesus arrived in Israel without the slightest fanfare. His birth mother, a teenage Jewish virgin named Mary, resided in the Galilee region of Palestine. The confusion surrounding the nature of her pregnancy caused others to label her an adulteress. She avoided the penalty of death by stoning because Joseph, her fiancé, claimed the child (Matthew 1:18-25).

Near the end of her pregnancy, Mary traveled with Joseph to Bethlehem in response to a government census decree (Matthew 2:22-23).

Because Joseph was of the lineage of Judah, he was required to register in Bethlehem, the city of David. Soon after Mary gave birth to Jesus in what was probably a cave among animals, she and Joseph escaped to Egypt with Jesus. An angel had warned them that to avoid a widespread infanticide commissioned by King Herod they must flee to Egypt immediately and not go home to Nazareth (Matthew 2:13-23).

I share these details with you because they represent one of my first encounters with information from the New Testament that significantly challenged my thinking. I was intrigued by the circumstances surrounding Jesus' arrival and how He was unnoticed by nearly everyone at the time. But far more importantly, I was struck by how the entire order of events concerning Jesus' birth fit squarely on the predictions outlined in the prophecies:

- The Messiah would be born in Bethlehem (Micah 5:2).
- He would be a descendent of the tribe of Judah (Genesis 49:10).
- He would be born of a virgin (Isaiah 7:14).
- Foreign kings would travel to pay homage to Him (Psalm 72:10-11).
- Children would be slaughtered in an effort to kill Him (Jeremiah 31:15).
- He would be taken to Egypt to escape the slaughter (Hosea 11:1).

In the Old Testament, the prophets documented more than one hundred proofs to confirm the genuine nature of the future Messiah. In this way, people could verify the significance of these events as they occurred. Similar to the other types of prophecies, I was amazed to discover how these early Scriptures predicted with such amazing accuracy the events that would later occur concerning Jesus' arrival. Because of the timing and circumstances of Jesus' life, it appeared to me that He's the only person in history that fulfilled, explained, and carried out each of these prophecies.[28]

The Implications of a Divine Incarnation

As I continued to read, I began to recognize some of the real world impacts that took place as a result of Jesus becoming a man. By putting on human flesh, Jesus acquired a human intellect. He set Himself up to battle the same kinds of trials and temptations we experience. He also had eyes of flesh to view His neighbor, hands to touch lepers, and feet to walk along the Sea of Galilee. He experienced the full gamut of human emotions. As far as I could tell, for the first time, God is described in the Scriptures as facing man *as another man* and speaking to him face-to-face.

Emphasizing the fact that he was an eyewitness to Jesus' miraculous incarnation, John the apostle opened his first letter with these words:

> "That which was from the beginning, which we have heard, which we have seen with our eyes, which we have looked at and our hands have touched—this we proclaim concerning the Word of life. The life appeared; we have seen it and testify to it, and we proclaim to you the eternal life, which was with the Father and has appeared to us. We proclaim to you what we have seen and heard...."
>
> (1 JOHN 1:1-30)

John later wrote in his Gospel:

"The Word became flesh and made His dwelling among us. We have seen his glory, the glory of the one and only Son, who came from the Father...."

(JOHN 1:14)

In contrast to the expectations of the Jewish leaders, the extreme sub-ordinary way Jesus entered the world foretold His intention not to reign as an earthly king. Without a palace, royal chariot, or servants, I began to see how Jesus was laying the groundwork for a kingship of a different kind. I also began to understand how if Jesus had established Himself as a human king, He might not have been able to offer His message with the same effectiveness.

Jesus as a Boy

I found that the Gospels were conspicuously silent on the topic of Jesus' childhood and early adulthood. I did find out, however, that following the news of Herod's death, Mary and Joseph returned with Jesus to their home in Nazareth (Luke 2:3-9). On their way to Nazareth they passed by Jerusalem, possibly even stopping there.

Jerusalem was the site of the great Jewish Temple with its rituals. The famed city was home to learned rabbis and the center of Hebrew thinking. Jerusalem represented the heart of Jewish culture, history, and learning. Jewish families throughout the Roman Empire sent their brightest young boys to Jerusalem to study the Law under the great rabbis. Paul from Tarsus was one of those students. He was mentored by the famous Gamaliel (Acts 22:3). Accordingly, most all Jews of great influence graduated from a Jewish seminary in Jerusalem.

So I was surprised to find out that Jesus, the one the New Testament Scriptures claims is the Jewish Messiah, never participated in this Ivy

League of Jewish-styled education. He chose, instead, not to differentiate Himself in class or by formal education. He remained a carpenter's son in a village so obscure it was not located on many maps of the time. He would fulfill His role as God's messenger from among the people, not in a rabbinic classroom.

Generally speaking, many Jews regarded Galileans as commoners with an inferior education. Galileans tended to speak in dialects of Hebrew rather than the purest form of the language. People residing in small villages received the least respect. Speaking lightheartedly after he first heard that Jesus was from Nazareth, Nathanael said, "Nazareth! Can anything good come from there?" (John 1:46).

I found the Gospels' silence concerning Jesus' childhood to break ever so briefly in Luke 2:39-52 to tell us that after returning to Nazareth from Egypt, Jesus "grew and became strong; he was filled with wisdom, and the grace of God was upon him." The remaining information documented an incident when Jesus was twelve. Mary and Joseph assumed Jesus was with friends or family in a traveling caravan returning to Galilee from a Passover celebration in Jerusalem. Upon finding their assumptions incorrect, they anxiously returned to Jerusalem. Three days later they found Jesus, "sitting among the teachers, listening to them and asking them questions. Everyone who heard Him was amazed at His understanding and His answers" (Luke 2:46-47).

Jesus: A Man of Intense Emotions

The Gospels record how many years later, at around age thirty, Jesus' life took a dramatic turn. It all began when Jesus, with few words of persuasion, convinced twelve men to leave their livelihood and families to follow Him. These recruits represented a mixture of otherwise ordinary and unsophisticated Galileans. Only one, Judas of Iscariot, hailed from Judea. Fishermen, farmers, and a tax collector among them, they represented everyday people. No scholars were among the group.

Noting their vast differences, Dietrich Bonhoeffer opined "No power in the world could have united these men for a common task, save the call of Jesus."[29]

From my reading of material outside the Scriptures I learned how many theologians throughout the years have categorized Jesus' apostles as dense, mistake prone, and untalented. But the more I read about them, the more I saw them differently. These men, although simple, seemed unspoiled by the world's system of wealth, power, and the prejudice that tends to creep into the hearts of those who pursue extensive education. I began to see the apostles as men that Jesus thought were more likely to understand and be willing to receive the great love the Gospels claimed He offered. They didn't fit the description Jesus gave of those who found it more difficult to enter heaven than for a camel to crawl through the eye of a needle (Matthew 19:23-26). Despite their future missteps causing some theologians to label them as Jesus' ragtag band of unpromising recruits, it seems Jesus chose His friends less for their intellect and more for their clear hearts and ability to give and receive love.

In human terms, I think of kings or other royalty, like Princess Anne, as stoic, always presenting themselves with a dignified, unemotional front. On the other hand, I found Jesus to be an *intensely* emotional being. The Gospels describe Jesus as one who cried openly upon seeing the pain and anguish of others. He grieved over those who exhibited hard hearts. He reeled with anger at the moneychangers and their disrespect for all that the Temple represented. He displayed compassion for the sick and lame. His joy seemed at its highest when He was surrounded by children who accepted and loved Him freely.

Jesus didn't hide His emotions. His apparent love for all was on full display.

One incident reflecting the openness and depth of Jesus' emotions struck me more than any other. After the meal at the Last Supper, while reclining with His disciples, Jesus said one of them would betray Him.

While the Gospel narrative focuses mainly on the betrayal and who would carry this out, the deep relationship Jesus had with one of His disciples forms a significant subplot to the story.

> "When Jesus had said this, He became troubled in spirit, and testified and said, 'Truly, truly, I say to you, that one of you will betray me.' The disciples began looking at one another, at a loss to know of which one He was speaking. *There was reclining on Jesus' bosom one of his disciples, whom Jesus loved.* So Simon Peter gestured to him, and said to him, 'Tell us who it is of whom He is speaking.' *He, leaning back thus on Jesus' bosom,* said to Him, 'Lord, who is it?'"
>
> (JOHN 13:21-25 NAS, emphasis mine)

Remarkable! After Jesus and His twelve disciples finished eating, one of the disciples rested his head on Jesus' chest. The implications as to the depth of their relationship, the interaction of their minds and souls, as well as the degree of their confidence in each other's love astounded me.

This scene reminds me in many ways of my relationship with my lifelong friend, Tom. My memory doesn't reach back farther than our friendship. We met as three years olds. Attending the same schools through high school graduation, we laughed, cried, argued, and had all kinds of fun together. We were not identical. But we both held an unwavering commitment, tested by time, to protect and enjoy each other. We cherished and jealously guarded our close friendship.

Just a few weeks before Tom's untimely death, I visited him in Daytona Beach, Florida, where he had recently accepted a position in a prestigious law firm as a tax attorney. Not knowing how to fully express with words how we missed each other over the previous weeks, we proceeded to wrestle at something less than three-quarters speed. It was more along the lines of a lengthy, active hug. But as deep as our open display of love for each other revealed, neither Tom nor I loved like the Jesus I was reading about. He was the master lover.

The open display of affection between Jesus and John was not what I expected. It certainly wasn't the type of behavior we see between an earthly king and one of his subordinates. But it was clear from my reading of the Gospels that Jesus was a completely different kind of King, a divine King, who always chose intimacy over formality. His open affection for a cherished friend represented a significant breakthrough in my learning about His true personality.

Many passages in the Gospels describe Jesus as a man who sought the hearts of others. Those willing to do the same were high on His list. He knew those who hesitated to seek and engage in deep relationships would fail to understand the unique opportunity He presented. And so, it is along these lines that Jesus chose His friends.

Jesus' Public Life

After Jesus chose His disciples, the Gospels go on to describe how Jesus would soon begin His time of openly proclaiming who He was in the kingdom of God to those outside of His small group of hand-picked followers. His public life came to be characterized by miracles, including healing the sick, as well as teaching the principles of the kingdom. I soon came to realize that Jesus' life would be characterized in two ways: His performance of miracles, including healing the sick, and His teaching the principles of His kingdom.

The Gospels indicate that a short time after Jesus called His disciples to follow Him, they attended a wedding together in the small village of Cana near Nazareth (John 2:1-11). When the wine ran out too early, Jesus' mother asked Him to help. Somehow she must have known He was capable of producing the wine that would save the wedding party from embarrassment. But Jesus seemed to know that once He performed His first miracle, word of it would bring droves of people in search of His help. There would be no turning back the tide.

Jesus first responded to His mother with a question, "Woman, why do you involve me?' (John 2:4). As if He knew what her response would be, He went on to support His desire not to be involved. "My hour has not yet come," He said. Mary said nothing further; but after weighing the consequences, Jesus changed water into wine.

From that point forward, the Gospels assert that Jesus exerted His supernatural powers by healing with such frequency that the Gospel writers couldn't document every incident. John stated in the final verse of his Gospel that, "Jesus did many other things as well. If every one of them were written down, I suppose that even the whole world would not have room for the books that would be written" (John 21:25). But despite His tendency to perform many miracles, Jesus denied the request of those who displayed a "show-me-and-I'll-believe-it" attitude. Instead, He unveiled His supernatural powers when and how He deemed appropriate to prove His deity and proclaim His message.

The Gospel writers assert that Jesus performed all kinds of various miracles including causing the blind to see, the deaf to hear, and the lame to walk. On three occasions they claim He even turned back death.[30] Fitting no particular pattern, some people were healed after He touched them. A woman somehow was healed simply by touching Jesus' garments (Mark 5:21-43). Another recipient of Jesus' healing power was not even in His presence (John 4:46-54). On at least four separate occasions, Jesus healed blind men.[31] In one circumstance, Jesus simply spoke (Mark 10:46-54). On another occasion, He formed mud with His spittle and applied the mud to the victim's eyes (John 9:6). Upon washing in the manner Jesus prescribed, the blind man's sight was restored. In a third instance, Jesus spat directly on the blind person's eyes (Mark 8:22-26).

No disease or physical ailment was beyond Jesus' ability to cure.[32] He cleansed lepers (Matthew 8:1-4), healed a paralytic (Matthew 9:1-8), restored a severed ear (Luke 22:49-51), healed an epileptic boy (Matthew 17:14-16), and gave hearing and speech to a deaf mute (Matthew 9:32-34).

Jesus' command over the natural elements was evidenced by His calming a raging storm and walking on water (Mark 6:45-52).

After thinking about this for some time, I determined that despite maintaining the apparent power to do so, Jesus' goal was not to solve all of the world's physical ills. That's not what the Gospels say He came to do. I came to the conclusion that through His miracles Jesus hoped to achieve three objectives. First, it appeared He came to give people the message that God loved them. Secondly, like Moses, Elijah, and the prophets before Him, one of Jesus' goals was to verify His true identity. Citing the miracles occurring at His direction, Jesus made His claim that He was the Son of God (John 10:37-38). And thirdly, it appeared to me that Jesus performed miracles to show us that one day God will relieve us of all our burdens.

Jesus' Early Teachings

Following the first wave of His miraculous healings, Jesus rode a tremendous surge of popularity. As word of what Jesus was doing spread throughout the region, people began traveling from far away to seek miracles for their needs. In the span of a few short days, an enormous crowd began following Him wherever He went (Matthew 4:25). These crowds formed the audience Jesus first spoke to concerning His kingdom. At one point, on a grassy hill above the Sea of Galilee, Jesus gathered the crowd and began teaching with wisdom and authority no one had ever witnessed before.

From the beginning, Jesus established themes that would reverberate throughout His public ministry. Speaking against the many counterfeit philosophies woven so deeply into man's thinking, the first concept He addressed was the notion that the rich and powerful hold special favor in God's eyes. To the surprise of His audience, Jesus started listing those who were "blessed" by including some who maintained the greatest needs.

> "Blessed are the poor in spirit....
> Blessed are those who mourn....
> Blessed are you when people insult you, persecute you
> and falsely say all kinds of evil against you because
> of me."
>
> (MATTHEW 5:3-11)

Throughout this teaching, Jesus explained how His kingdom and God's love are available to everyone. He assured those in the crowd who considered themselves the lost causes of the world that God holds great compassion for *all* people. He told them that God sees each person as His precious child and wants everyone to come home to Him.

He warned the rich and poor people in the crowd alike saying:

> "Do not store up for yourselves treasures on earth,
> where moth and vermin destroy, and where thieves
> break in and steal. But store up for yourselves treasures
> in heaven, where moths and vermin do not destroy,
> and where thieves do not break in and steal. For where
> your heart is, there your heart will be also."
>
> (MATTHEW 6:19-21)

Clearly, Jesus was insisting that God doesn't favor anyone on the basis of his or her social or economic status or the lack of such status.

A Different Way of Teaching: the Parables

Although Jesus' teaching would take many forms, I found that His manner of storytelling set Him apart. Using images from the everyday life of His audiences, Jesus' parables explained the truths of His kingdom.

Some stories illustrated the importance of God's kingdom when compared to all other issues in life. "The kingdom of heaven is like treasure hidden in a field," Jesus said. "When a man found it, he hid it again, and then in his joy went and sold all he had and bought that field. Again, the kingdom of heaven is like a merchant looking for fine pearls. When he found one of great value, he went away and sold everything he had and bought it" (Matthew 13:46).

Other parables Jesus told illustrated God's unyielding and unconditional love. Jesus once spoke of a shepherd who left ninety-nine sheep in the open country and searched for one lost sheep until he found it. Also, He told about a woman who lost a silver coin. She lit a lamp, scoured the house, and let nothing interrupt her search until she recovered the missing coin. Subsequently, she invited her neighbors to rejoice with her. Similarly, Jesus indicated there is much rejoicing in heaven over every lost person who comes home to Him.

A parable Jesus told about a lost son impacted me the most. For some reason, it grabbed hold of something deep inside me and wouldn't let it go. As the story goes, the youngest of two sons asked his father to give him his inheritance while he was still young. With his inheritance in hand, the young man left home with no intention of returning. Far from home, he squandered his father's money on wild living. After feeding pigs to get money to buy food, the wayward son realized that even his father's hired hands lived better than he. So he set out to ask his father to hire him as a servant. "But while he was still a long way off, his father saw him and was filled with compassion for him; he ran to his son, and threw his arms around him and kissed him" (Luke 15:11-32). And a great celebration ensued. The father's response to his returning son illustrates God's forgiveness, joy, and acceptance of those who return to Him.

My first reading of this story required only a few moments, but it took much longer to ponder all its implications. The father's unrelenting and unconditional love for his son painted a picture in my mind. I used this mental portrait and the lessons I learned from the other parables as guideposts to help me interpret the rest of Scripture.

The Beckoning

During my first reading of the New Testament, I found Jesus' teachings more interesting than I anticipated. I found the parables even more intriguing. But one of the most significant points in my investigation came when I started to see the connection between what Jesus had been saying and what would happen when He entered Jerusalem for the last time.

In the next chapter we'll continue our look at Jesus as one of God's messengers. We'll concentrate on the events that took place in the final week of His life—the week I now believe to be the most significant in all of human history.

Think It Through! Talk It Over!

1. What did you know about Jesus when you were a child?
2. What were your earliest impressions of Jesus?
3. How have your impressions of Jesus changed from childhood until now? What caused them to change?
4. What do you believe was the main reason for Jesus' birth?
5. What do you think gift-giving at Christmas represents. Explain.
6. Why do you agree or disagree that there had to be something special or powerful about Jesus that persuaded the disciples to leave all and follow Him?

7. On a scale of 0 to 10, how willing are you to follow Jesus? Explain your answer.

8. Can you relate in any way to the story of the wayward son (the Prodigal Son)? If so, how?

9. What, if anything, do you find attractive about Jesus' earthly ministry?

10. What do you believe was the main reason Jesus died on the Cross?

GOD'S MESSENGER:
JESUS' FAREWELL TOUR

"He was despised and rejected by mankind . . . Surely
he took up our pain and bore our suffering . . . he was
pierced for our transgressions . . . the punishment that
brought us peace was on him, and by his wounds we
are healed."

ISAIAH 53:3-5

To view Michael's introductory video for Chapter 5,
please go to www.michaelminot.com/thebeckoning

*W*hen musicians and singers announce their retirement, some
give their fans a farewell tour or concert. Symbolic gestures

may include cutting the strings of a guitar at the end of the last song or auctioning off the group's musical instruments following the final concert. Retiring athletes, touring artifact exhibits, and even some politicians get into the act as well. On a local level, when someone leaves employment, often a "going away" party is given to wish the departing person well.

To me, the most significant of all farewells during my lifetime was that of evangelist Billy Graham. At a time when the world was still healing from the devastation of World War II and before Elvis Presley recorded his first song, Billy Graham launched what became a decades-long world tour from Los Angeles in 1949. Spanning 185 countries and reaching more than 210 million people through his stadium-style crusades, this Christian warrior also published more than 20 books, wrote a weekly newspaper column published around the world, and reached millions more through radio. For more than 50 years, this man of impeccable integrity preached his powerful message of God's love.

Putting bookends on his life of crusades, in 2004 Billy came back to Los Angeles one last time. He spoke for four nights at the 92,000-seat Rose Bowl. As his final farewell, the 86-year-old evangelist then went to New York's Flushing Meadows Park in June 2005 to give what would be his final talks. Reporters came from around the globe to cover the Crusade—more than 700 in all.[33] With an underlying message that never varied, Mr. Graham offered the perspective that, "Our world is constantly changing but the needs of our hearts remain the same, and so does God's power to transform our lives and give us hope for the future."[34]

After reading through the Gospels, I learned that similar to Billy Graham, Jesus had a farewell tour of his own. But the end of His tour would be unlike any other. I also determined that the pinnacle point of the Scriptures is the final week of Jesus' life. This chapter, therefore, is dedicated to giving you some of the details that were influential in helping me understand the significance of Jesus' last days.

Jesus' Farewell Tour

Jesus' followers missed the fact He began organizing His own farewell tour when He sent seventy of His disciples, two-by-two, into every city where He'd soon be going (Luke 10:1). The role John the Baptizer fulfilled by preparing the way for Jesus at the beginning of His public life, the seventy would perform at its end. But Jesus' followers must have sensed something unusual was occurring. For the past three years, Jesus had taught primarily from Galilee, with an occasional visit to Jerusalem or other cities. Often, people had traveled long distances _to see Him_. In never-before-type fashion, Jesus now planned to visit the people _where they lived, in their own cities._

To complete this tour of no less than thirty-five localities, Jesus must have started His journey at least six to nine months before its conclusion. For these many months, He traveled in a zigzag fashion throughout Galilee, Samaria, Judea, and the Diaspora (a region of cities located mostly in modern-day Jordan). Jesus timed the beginning of His tour so that He would arrive at Jerusalem, His final stop, in time for following year's spring Passover celebration.

The way the Gospels described the situation, this journey certainly didn't look or feel like a farewell tour. Jesus was in His early to mid-thirties. He was in good health, considering the extensive demands of such an aggressive travel schedule. So, too, His popularity with the people was rising, not diminishing. He continued to heal blind people, leapers, and others, just as before. He even raised Lazarus from the dead. By the end of this nationwide tour, His fame had reached its zenith. Almost everyone between Galilee and Jerusalem who hadn't traveled to see Him before now had the opportunity to experience His compassion firsthand. They set aside whatever rumors they'd heard about His teaching and healings in favor of face-to-face experiences with Him.

After examining the Gospel accounts of Jesus' life numerous times, including what took place during His tour of cities, I began to wonder whether I could be reading something other than a random, unscripted drama. The way the events in Jesus' life lined up with what would soon occur in Jerusalem made it seem like a carefully planned, deliberate series of events was under way. I was taken back by the clarity by which Jesus knew what was about to happen.

> "Now they were on the road on their way to Jerusalem, Jesus walking in the lead, and were filled with awe and fear as they followed. And again, taking the Twelve aside along the way, he began to tell them the things that would happen to him, saying to them, 'Behold, we are going up to Jerusalem, and everything written by the prophets concerning the Son of man will be fulfilled. For he will be betrayed to the chief priests and the scribes, and they will condemn him to death and deliver him up to the Gentiles to crucify him. And he will be mocked and treated shamefully and spit upon, and they will scourge him and put him to death; but the third day he will rise again.'
>
> Yet the disciples understood none of these things."
> (MATTHEW 20:17-19; MARK 10:32-34; LUKE 18:31-34)[35]

Putting all this together, I started to entertain the possibility that not only all the circumstances of Jesus' life but all of the history outlined in the Old Testament had prepared the groundwork for what was about to occur at the end of Jesus' journey.

The Crowds in Bethany

After many months of traveling, Jesus' arrived at Bethany, a town on the eastern outskirts of Jerusalem (Matthew 21:1-11). By invitation, He had previously eaten many meals and even stayed overnight there. Jesus would later choose Bethany as the place He would be last seen. He would bless His followers there one last time before ascending into heaven. On this occasion, however, Bethany was the place from which Jesus would enter Jerusalem to end His farewell tour and begin His final week on earth.

Local people and travelers alike began showing their affection for Jesus at Bethany. One after another they loudly acclaimed Him as the first Jewish prophet to appear in 400 years. Have you ever joined in a standing ovation at the end of a performance? Usually, the actions of one or two inspire others to join in. I imagine the same was true as Jesus began passing through Bethany.

A small number of His appreciative followers began shouting their praises and likely sang Jewish victory songs like that in Psalm 118. "Blessed is He who comes in the name of the LORD" (Psalm 118:26). As more and more people joined the crowd, some greeted Jesus as if He was royalty. They began laying their coats and palm branches in His path. (Matthew 21:8). All the noise and activity continued to draw even more people. A wave of exuberant activity continued to build along the two-mile stretch from Bethany to Jerusalem.

But Jesus wasn't riding a white stallion. Nor was He standing in a chariot pulled by a team of horses as an earthly king wanting to display his power would do. He chose to present Himself meekly by riding on a donkey (Mark 11:2-7).

Hearing the commotion, some of the Pharisees made their way to the crowd. They bristled at how the people were loudly proclaiming Jesus as a prophet or king. After scoffing at Jesus for accepting their praise, one of the Pharisees demanded that He instruct the crowd to stop calling Him a king. Jesus responded by saying, "If they keep quiet, the stones along the road will burst into cheers!" (Luke 19: 39-40, TLB).

If any question existed before, these indignant Pharisees now knew that Jesus, without their endorsement, claimed to be the King of the Jews. Since the Pharisees, too, were Jews, this meant He claimed to be king over them as well.

Though the week had just started, the tension was already building.

Difficulty Following Jesus

While reading these passages, I noticed not only the different ways people greeted Jesus but also that their willingness to consider what He was saying fell mostly along party lines. Many, but certainly not all, became infected by the stern demands of a rule-based mentality. The rules imposed by the religious leaders governed how they ate, drank, and otherwise carried out their lives. Rituals for many occasions were spelled out to the letter.

In response to what the religious leaders expected, some people did as they were told. They were slaves to detail. "I must follow the rules," some thought, "because if I do, then God will be pleased with me." But trying to live by the letter of those all-encompassing mandates suffocated the hearts of many.

Ironically, one of Jesus' stories illustrates the striking contrast between how His worshipful followers received His teachings and how the religious leaders received it. The parable mentions how seed doesn't always fall on good soil. Sometimes it falls on roads, or on rocky soil, or among thorns, none of which is suitable for growth. Jesus explained:

> "The seed is the word of God; *the Sower* is sowing the *Word*. When anyone hears the Word of the Kingdom and does not comprehend it, then at once Satan, the

wicked one, comes and snatches away what has been sown in his heart, lest he should believe and be saved. This is he who received seed upon the roadside.

"And likewise he who received seed on the rocky places, this is he who hears the word and it was received gladly; yet he has no root in himself, and the leaves and continues only a little while. Then later, when adversity arises, or persecution on account of the Word, he is caused to stumble immediately, and falls away.

"He also received seed among the thorns is he who, on hearing the Word, goes away; and the cares of this world and the pleasures of life, the seductiveness of riches, and passionate desires for other things, enter in and choke the Word and it is made unfruitful—it brings no fruit to completion.

"But he who received seed upon the good soil is he who, hearing the Word in an honest and good heart, welcomes and understands it and holds it fast, and with patience bears fruit in deed and brings fruit, some thirtyfold, some sixty, and some hundred fold."
(MATTHEW 13:18-23; MARK 4:13-20; LUKE 8:11-15)[36]

Jesus accused those "superior in learning" of stumbling over their own academic pursuits. They failed to see beyond their scholastic exercises and recognize what was most important. As I read about the Pharisees' reaction to Jesus, it appeared to me that some of them would rather analyze the proverbial last drop of water in the desert for its structural qualities rather than drink it for its life-sustaining nourishment. They also seemed to elevate the Scriptures and their man-made rules above the God they claimed to serve. In their dissections, they strained to capture every nuance of the law.

It seemed plain from my reading that the message Jesus offered turned the religious leaders' perspective of life upside down. From the beginning of His public life, Jesus emphasized that true life comes from a life of love, not from a rigid behavioral code or rituals. And love is made greater by serving others, not toiling to satisfy our self-interests.

> "Whoever wants to become great among you must be your servant, and whoever wants to be first must be your slave—just as the Son of Man did not come to be served, but to serve, and to give his life as a ransom for many."
>
> (MATTHEW 20:26-28)

Again, on another occasion Jesus said:

> "The greatest among you will be your servant. For those who exalt themselves will be humbled, and those who humble themselves will be exalted."
>
> (MATTHEW 23:11-12)

Jesus never emphasized the letter of the law. In fact, His objectors questioned why He so often refused to abide by the rules created by the religious leaders. Indeed, it seemed to me that the entire theme of Jesus' teaching was anti-ritualistic. Instead of focusing on outward appearances or whether a person's deeds fit an accepted pattern, Jesus addressed the condition of the heart. He pointed out how man-made moral codes governing people's behavior fail to help us satisfy our deepest longings.

The Final Straw

From my reading, it appeared that one of the most critical events of the week occurred the day after Jesus arrived at Bethany. The Gospels indicate that on that day Jesus entered the Temple in Jerusalem and observed merchants selling animals for sacrifices there. One section was set up with tables for those exchanging money. Jesus witnessed how the merchants, under the supervision of the Temple priests, charged extravagant prices for suitable sacrificial animals. The moneychangers, too, collected exorbitant fees. Jesus considered the practice of extorting money from peasant travelers seeking to purify themselves at the Temple as the ultimate hypocrisy. After observing these fraudulent practices, He concluded that His Father's house had been turned into a "den of thieves" (Matthew 21:12-13).

Outraged, "Jesus made a whip from some ropes and chased them all out of the Temple. He drove out the sheep and cattle, scattered the money changers' coins over the floor, and turned over their tables. Then, going over to the people who sold doves, he told them, 'Get these things out of here. Stop turning my Father's house into a marketplace!'" (John 2:15-16, NLT). The Pharisees were infuriated. Though Jesus had chastised them in the past, causing such a scene in the Temple was considered the height of disrespect. It pushed the Pharisees over the brink. The fuse of the Pharisees' time bomb was now lit.

When I first read the account of what happened in the Temple, I failed to put together how the rage of the Pharisees fit perfectly into God's plan. But I wasn't alone. No one witnessing these events foresaw how God's plan to establish His forgiveness of mankind was actually the story of how Jesus would soon die for all of mankind.

Jesus' Final Steps

As I continued reading, I learned that during His first few days in Jerusalem Jesus attracted larger crowds and spoke to more people than at any other time. Scores of people from around the Roman Empire, some who never heard Him before, were in awe as they listened to Jesus explain the truths of God's kingdom in ways they never heard before (Luke 19:48). Some began to view Him as a prophet. At one point, crowds in the Temple area began singing, "Hosanna to the Son of David" (Matthew 21:9), a phrase reserved for the Messiah.

Many could not stop talking about Him. He became the buzz of Jerusalem. By Thursday, His popularity had soared beyond celebrity status. However, unlike the attitude held by the enthusiastic crowd, the mainline religious establishment burned with anger, fueled by the realization they had been replaced.

In a way that nobody but Jesus could comprehend, the contrast of views held by the people and the religious leaders would soon produce dire consequences for Jesus. Again, with a level of accuracy I found stunning, here's how the prophecies of the Old Testament foretold the final sequence of Jesus' life:

- The Messiah would enter Jerusalem riding a donkey. (Zechariah 9:9)
- He would be betrayed by a friend. (Psalm 41:9)
- He would be sold for thirty pieces of silver. (Zechariah 11:12-13)
- He would be silent in front of His accusers. (Isaiah 53:7)
- He would be beaten, mocked, and spat upon. (Isaiah 50:6)
- Men would gamble for His clothing. (Psalm 22:18)
- He would be crucified with criminals. (Isaiah 53:12)
- He would be raised from the dead. (Psalm 16:10, 11)

As I doubled back and read the Gospels a number of times, I came to realize how the circumstances surrounding Jesus' birth, life, and death fulfilled each of these messianic prophecies and dozens more. There were so many detailed predictions that it seemed, statistically speaking, impossible for anyone to fulfill them all by accident. And considering how detailed the prophecies were, I was surprised that the religious leaders failed to recognize their error. It seems all they could see was their base of power being threatened.

But even Jesus' followers failed to see how perfectly Jesus' life fulfilled every messianic prophecy. Only after the resurrection, and with the help of hindsight, His followers finally matched all the prophets' predictions with the events of Jesus' life. Almost 2,000 Easters later, many people continue to struggle with the precision which Jesus' life fulfilled the prophecies.

The Passover Meal

The mismatched attitudes between the crowds and the religious leaders formed the backdrop for what would happen on Thursday night and the early hours of the next morning. Jesus began this historic Thursday evening by sharing the Passover meal with His apostles (Luke 22:7-23). But no one celebrating this feast with Jesus realized how this most widely observed Jewish holiday would take on a far more significant meaning than that of Israel's redemption from Egypt.

The more I read the more I sensed that Jesus' footsteps were in lockstep with what God the Father planned from the beginning. Each stride Jesus took on His way to the city of David and the Temple was synchronized with a timeline that had reached its final hours.

But it seemed that no one except Jesus understood that the remaining hours of this Passover festival would be His last on earth. He tried one last time to explain to His closest followers what lay squarely in front of Him and that He must leave them. But they still were unable to understand (John 16:16-22). Highlighting the blinding optimism held by Jesus' followers, N.T. Wright comments,

> "Nobody in this period supposed that the Messiah would suffer, let alone die. Indeed, that was the very opposite of normal expectations. The Messiah was supposed to be leading

the triumphant fight against Israel's enemies, not dying at their hands."[37]

Chuck Colson described the confusing irony of Jesus, as the Messiah, giving Himself up in this way:

"...all through human history, as far back as recorded time and doubtless before, kings, princes, tribal chiefs, presidents, and dictators, have sent their subjects into battle to die for them. Only once in human history has a king not sent his subjects to die for him, but instead, died for his subjects. This is the King who introduces His Kingdom that cannot be shaken, because this King reigns eternally."[38]

Like the calm before a tsunami, these moments during the Passover meal were warm and tender. But in an iconic move, shortly after the meal, Jesus intentionally put Himself in harm's way. Today, many years after my initial investigation, I've come to the conclusion that these hours represent some of the darkest moments in human history.

Betrayed, Scorned, Beaten, and Crucified

Later that evening, after being betrayed by one of His friends (Luke 22:1-54), Jesus endured the humiliation of a mock trial at the hands of the religious leaders in the early hours of Friday morning. Driven senseless by their raging envy and fear of losing their "place," they falsely accused Jesus, ridiculed Him, beat Him, repeatedly punched Him in the face while He was blindfolded, and spat upon Him. When dawn finally came, they dragged Jesus before Pilate, the Roman curator of Judea, demanding that He be crucified. More than once Pilate proclaimed that Jesus was not guilty of any crime (John 18:28–19:16). But when Pilate announced his intention to release Jesus, the angry lynch mob assembled by the religious leaders came unglued and began shouting. In an attempt to appease the angry crowd, Pilate ordered Jesus to be flogged (John 19:1).

Using whips made with chords of tasseled leather holding sharp stones, the Roman soldiers ripped the skin from Jesus' back, arms, and legs. The level of Jesus' suffering must have exceeded the profane. It's not hard to imagine after all this inhumane brutality how Jesus' body reflected the description given in Isaiah 52:14: "many...were appalled at him—his appearance was so disfigured beyond that of any human being and his form marred beyond human likeness."

After Jesus was beaten to the point of being half dead, Pilate returned to the crowd with the renewed intention of releasing Him. His thinking was that the brutal torture of Jesus would satisfy His enemies. But as Pilate soon learned, they were far from satisfied. Not content with any outcome other than death, they began shouting, "Crucify him! Crucify him!" (Mark 15:12-14). Unrelenting, the angry mob threatened Pilate saying, "If you let this man go, you are no friend of Caesar" (John 19:12).

Soon, the escalating pressure tactics employed by the crowd caused Pilate to crack. Apparently to avoid whatever repercussions came with permitting a riot, Pilate capitulated to the howling mob and ordered Jesus to be crucified. As if enough tragedy had not yet occurred, a completely innocent man was sentenced to die at the hands of both His own people and the Roman government.

Just outside the city walls at about 9 AM on Friday, morning soldiers hammered nails nearly the size of railroad spikes through Jesus' hands and feet. Jesus hung on the cross enduring excruciating pain for several hours. During those hours, many jeered as they passed by. "Hey Jesus, _save yourself!_ If you are the Son of God," they scoffed. The priests of the Temple, scribes, and other elders, also relished the opportunity to mock the apparently defenseless Jesus. Not to be outdone, the Roman soldiers standing guard joined in showing their disrespect. They shouted, "If you are the king of the Jews, save yourself!" One of the criminals hanging alongside Jesus hurled insults too (Luke 23:36-39).

But one small light shone brightly in this hideously dark place. Unlike the first criminal, a second displayed a different outlook during these final minutes of life. Sober to the fact his life's story stood against all that was good, he maintained the wisdom and presence of mind to ask Jesus to forgive him. "Jesus," he requested, "remember me when you come into your kingdom" (Luke 23:42).

I read earlier how many times in Jesus' life, He met people who'd made a mess of their lives. A woman with five husbands; Zacchaeus, the unscrupulous tax collector; and a woman caught in adultery; among others. With sincerity in their hearts they had sought forgiveness. Regardless of their life's circumstances or the degree of their poor choices, Jesus offered forgiveness to all who approached Him with simple faith and sincere hearts. These last moments of His life were no different. As He had done in every similar occasion before, with instant forgiveness in His heart, Jesus told the repentant criminal, "Today you will be with me in paradise" (Luke 23:43).

The Eternal Impact of Jesus' Death

Within the events of this week lies the answer to one of my long-standing questions. I knew when I entered my investigation that I needed an answer to the question of *why* Jesus, as the person who is claimed to be God incarnate, came to earth? Why would *God* lower Himself to a human stature, and place Himself in our environment, only to endure such great pain? What I discovered is that the ultimate reason for Jesus becoming human was not to teach or perform astonishing miracles, although He impacted thousands in those ways. According to many passages in the New Testament, He came for a larger, more lasting purpose. He came to save mankind. And He would do so not through His life but by His death.

Max Lucado, in his book, *He Chose The Nails* made these observations:

> "The crowd (mistakenly) concluded that the purpose of the pounding was to skewer the hands of Christ to the beam. But they were only half-right. We can't fault them for missing the other half. They couldn't see it. But Jesus could. And heaven could. And we can.
>
> "Through the eyes of Scripture we see what others missed and what Jesus saw: "He canceled the record that contained the charges against us. He took it and destroyed it by nailing it to His cross"
>
> (COLOSSIANS 2:14 NLT).[39]

After living through what he first thought was the catastrophe of Jesus' death, the apostle Peter later described what he learned about the significance of Jesus' death. He wrote: "He Himself bore our sins in His body on the cross, so that we might die to sins and live for righteousness; by his wounds you have been healed" (1 Peter 2:24).

After putting all the pieces together, I realized that the Scriptures portrayed Jesus' death as accomplishing what we or the Jewish sacrificial system of animals could never fulfill. By dying for us, Jesus not only accepted the punishment for our waywardness, but made it possible for us to be free from all their entanglements. He voluntarily came to reverse the role He held as the one who *received* man's sacrifices in favor of *becoming* the perfect, final sacrifice for man. According to the Scriptures, the crucifixion of Jesus stands as the focal point of the story, the centerpiece of God's plan to liberate mankind. Only Jesus held the power to set things right, completing all that was necessary to reconcile man to Himself. This was His mission, His burden to bear.

Since becoming a believer, many people have asked me, "Why did all of Jesus' unspeakable suffering play such a purposeful and necessary part in God's plan. Couldn't God's goal of liberating us be accomplished in some other, less painful way?" My answer is: *apparently not*. Somehow, the precise circumstances of Jesus' life and death provided the necessary means for the Son of God to secure the keys to our deliverance. Somehow, as Jesus stretched out His arms to be nailed to the cross, He accomplished everything necessary on God's part to restore our relationship with Him.

Consider also what Tim Keller wrote in his book *The Reason For God* regarding the significance of Jesus' death:

"The founders of every other major religion essentially came as teachers, not as saviors. They came to say: 'Do this and you will find the divine.' But Jesus came essentially as a Savior rather than a teacher... Jesus says: 'I am the divine come to *you*, to do what you could not do for yourselves.' The Christian message is that we are saved not by our record, but by Christ's record."[40]

The Beckoning

From my research into the Gospels, I gained an understanding of the purpose of Jesus' life that I never had before.

Of course, I didn't pretend to understand all the details. But I sensed I'd acquired a good sense of what the primary pieces were and how they fit together. This was a story of a supernatural worldview that I was forced to admit had far more historical and real world underpinnings than I ever knew. Not only the story of Jesus' life and the amazing way it linked to the Hebrew prophecies, but I was astonished at the way the Scriptures explained the story of mankind through what happened to Jesus.

I sensed something had changed. By now I was *fully* engaged. The ground underneath me felt like it was beginning to shake. My desire to know more had encountered a massive growth spurt. I knew that I was incapable of letting go of this issue prematurely. Eventually, I'd stand on my research and declare my atheism more confidently than ever, or, I'd be a repentant soul to some entirely new way of thinking and living.

But many issues remain to be resolved. Next I decided to take on the perplexing, age-old issue of why there's so much suffering in the world.

Think It Through! Talk It Over!

1. What does it say about Jesus that He knew what would befall Him in Jerusalem?
2. What does it say about Him that He willingly went to Jerusalem to be crucified?
3. Why do you agree or disagree that Jesus died for you?
4. What one word do you think best characterizes Pilate's involvement in Jesus' crucifixion?
5. How would history have changed if Jesus had saved Himself from the Cross?
6. Why do you agree or disagree that love, not nails, kept Jesus on the Cross?
7. What do you think the crowds that welcomed Jesus to Jerusalem expected of Him?
8. Why do you agree or disagree that Jesus was a weak person?
9. Why do you think the religious leaders wanted Jesus to die on a cross?
10. Hypothetically, if you had been on a cross next to Jesus, what would you have said to Him? Why those words?

Chapter 6

GOD'S MESSENGER: THE EDUCATION OF PAIN

"Consider it pure joy, my brothers and sisters, whenever you face trials of many kinds, because you know that the testing of your faith produces perseverance. Let perseverance finish its work so that you may be mature and complete, not lacking anything."

JAMES 1:2-4

To view Michael's introductory video for Chapter 6, please go to www.michaelminot.com/thebeckoning

 grew unusually close to three friends when I was a young boy. In many ways, the four of us raised each other. Others marveled at our dedication to each other and depth of kinship. But against anything I ever thought possible, within ten years of high school graduation, my three friends died in separate incidents.

While covering a story in Africa, my friend David contracted a deadly tropical disease. Glenn sustained fatal injuries in a head-on car collision. Then, I received a call informing me that Tom, my lifelong best friend, lay comatose in a hospital from a severe car accident. After lengthy rehabilitation, Tom recouped physically. But later, he took his own life. Even though his body recuperated, trauma to the emotional centers of his brain failed to recover. Over a span of five short years, the unmanageable pain I experienced from losing my three do-anything-for-the-other friends took me to what I thought was the absolute bottom of life. Amidst the pain, questions flooded my mind such as "Why me? Of the four, why am I the only one to remain?" and "How can I pull through this debilitating pain?"

The experience of losing my friends represented a serious tipping point for me. I pondered my place in a world that doled out anguish and ruin in what appears to be such a random and extreme manner.

The Mystery and Challenge of Human Suffering

In the midst of my suffering I became more familiar with how other skeptics cite the daily array of suffering and destruction to support their beliefs. They highlight how acts of extreme cruelty and destruction unfold throughout the natural world. In the animal kingdom, living things prey on each other to survive. Raging wildfires cause great ruin. Earthquakes, tsunamis, and extreme weather, such as hurricanes and tornadoes, produce abrupt and massive devastation.

No human is immune from misery. Whether male or female, young or old, rich or poor, famous or unknown, nobody is exempt from having to face the consequences of living in this lost and broken world. Pain intersects the journey of all our lives. From this

I concluded that despite the natural beauty that's all around us, the world is a tragic place.

Later, when I began my investigation, I noted how theologians, too, debate the problem of pain and its relationship to the goodness of God. They examine the possible answers to questions such as, "In light of our extensive efforts to keep devastating disasters from occurring, why does God, with His unlimited powers, not prevent such tragedies?" and "If God is all loving, why would He not protect us from suffering?"

What I found from my research was that no one has ever resolved the issue of why we live in a world filled with such suffering. This leaves us with no absolute experts on the subject of pain. I did find, however, that the Scriptures often speak to the subject and offer some surprising explanations on this controversial issue. Thus, in this chapter I'll offer what I found the Scriptures to say about the topic as well as what I concluded at the end of my investigation. To get us started, let's first address the question of who's responsible for our suffering.

Cause of Pain: Corruption

In the midst of a mother's swelling pain after hearing the shocking news of her child's sudden death, the Scriptures indicate that it would be typical for Satan, the Enemy, to tempt her to cry out against God. When that mother receives her own diagnosis of an incurable disease, Satan encourages her to blame God and express resentment. He invites her to shout out against God saying, "Why should these disasters be happening *to me*? Why, God, did you not prevent my suffering? Where were you when my tragedies struck?"

To answer this mother's questions, the Scriptures assert that God didn't create evil and suffering. Further, the difficulties we experience in this life are not what God desired for us. Originally, He designed a place for us that was very good. In every way it was "Paradise." Here a harmonious relationship existed among all things. Unlike what we experience today, perfect unity once existed between us and the One who created us. God's original design, however, became dreadfully altered as a result of something gone wrong.

Humans have made a mess of things. Our choice to follow temptations instead of God's counsel and direction for us has altered the very fabric of our being. The lens we look through is different. We don't view ourselves, God, or each other in the same way. The early chapters in the book of Genesis indicate that Adam and Eve, our first parents, chose to follow their desires instead of God's. Consequently, they fractured their relationship with God and forfeited Paradise. This caused them to be thrust into an entirely different environment. Pain, not peace, characterized their new world.[41]

God Works for Our Redemption

From what I was reading, Satan stands ever ready to make us believe that God is always punishing us for making wrong turns. But this can't be true if as the Bible states, God is always aiming for our restoration. God isn't the source of life's sorrows, but He may permit them. Often we try to write a fairy tale story for ourselves believing God would never allow anything painful to happen in our lives. But if the words of the Bible are true, that's not reality.

From what the Scriptures say, God yearns to restore our beauty from the ashes we create. He desires to straighten what we have made crooked. He so desperately wants to restore what the locusts have eaten.

To accomplish this, God must bring about a process of regeneration. He must perform the difficult and arduous task of remaking our severely decayed beings. God desires more than anything for us to receive and respond to the never-ending invitations He issues. Unfortunately, as a result of our blindness, a highly potent stimulus may be necessary to bring us face-to-face with these staggering truths.

We'll begin our examination of how this process works by looking to creation and examining how one of nature's most destructive forces impacts the mightiest of trees.

The Wildfire Phenomenon

While growing in some cases to more than 300 feet with a base diameter of 40 feet, the Giant Sequoia tree of California sprouts from one of the tiniest seeds. So small, 3,000 of these seeds weigh merely an ounce.

In the early part of the twentieth century, a series of massive wildfires ravaged most of the Sequoias. In response to this devastation, the U.S. Forestry Service adopted an aggressive policy to suppress all forest fires. But studies performed decades after implementing the "No Burn" strategy revealed the unexpected. The unnatural suppression of fire impeded the vital role it played in both the germination and development of the Sequoia trees. In fact, the growth cycle of these magnificent trees depended on the major disturbances brought about by fire.

During the "No Burn" policy years, the forest floor became dense with vegetation. Dead and decaying debris accumulated unchecked. These conditions occurred as a direct consequence of suppressing the natural cleansing and regenerative processes performed by wildfires.

Without artificial restraint, cyclical fires burn away underbrush, thereby exposing the soil to the tiny Sequoia seeds that rarely sprout in dense vegetation. Heat from the flames stimulates the Sequoia pinecones to release their seeds. Burning also helps recycle nutrients into the soil. It clears the forest of shade-producing plants and trees blocking the sunlight the young seedlings so desperately need to grow. The cleansing effect of these recurring fires also keeps in check many pests that attack the trees. Most surprisingly, however, was how the periodic exposure to fire accelerated growth in the mature trees. Many of the trees exposed to the highest severity of fire experienced the largest and most sustained growth increases in the years following the fire.

How could this be? When we imagine the effects of intense fire on wood, images of blackened tree trunks, charred landscapes, and destruction come to mind. Yet, rather than making the trees weaker, occasional searing propels the Sequoias to new heights. In light of these findings, ecologists now realize that fire provides a natural benefit to woodland areas. Periodic burning should be prescribed, instead of suppressed, to stimulate much-needed and healthy changes. Could it be that the pains besieging humankind play a similar role in our lives?

Shock: the Human Earthquake

Living in an unreliable world, we struggle to create and maintain our own stable environment. We seek a pain-free existence. Like the Forestry Service, we too maintain a "No Burn" policy.

Regardless of this inclination, similar to the beneficial effect fires have on Sequoia trees, life's challenges redirect our considerations away from our daily routines and complacent thinking. I know from my own life that significant shifts in our *status quo* cause us to reassess where we are, where we've been, and where we're going.

When measuring how change influences our lives, circumstances causing us the greatest pain, particularly the unexpected, provide the most potent affect. Unprovoked terrorist bombings, the aftermath of natural disasters, the carnage of war, as well as the widespread risks associated with life-threatening diseases, all hold the power of distressing entire nations. On a personal level, the diagnosis of a terminal disease, an unannounced layoff, or the unexpected declaration of divorce, can leave us overwhelmed with grief. I say from my experiences that perhaps the most severe of our sorrows is the sudden death of someone we deeply love. The consuming grief one feels when faced with such a loss completely blots out the cares of life so important just a few moments before. But at the epicenter of any these crushing circumstances, no one continues their normal cadence. Maintaining a "business as usual" attitude is impossible.

Regardless of the type, when any life-altering event strikes, it exerts a transforming power on our personal outlook. Real tragedy interjects a different perspective to the previously acquired educational degrees, athletic triumphs, fame, net worth, and other worldly trophies we've acquired. Once the prime source of daily motivation, in an instant, all our self-centered goals and ambitions can be rendered meaningless.

The Power of Pain

My reading led me to believe that pain is far more central to the human story than I ever realized. A great number of people immunize themselves from the life-saving effect the truth provides. Turning their backs on the truth over and over again desensitizes them to the truth.

Many ignore the wonders found in nature and, likewise, never ponder God's truths in the Scriptures. People can effectively ignore these signposts if they so choose. But pain exerts a power that cannot be refused. Even those who deny God's presence are challenged by life's extreme moments. Unlike most other forces, pain cuts through our most fortified defenses and demands a response. It's as if we're compelled to stop and ask the important questions of life; the ones we've been postponing, or not asking at all. C.S. Lewis wrote:

"… pain insists upon being attended to. God whispers to us in our pleasures, speaks in our conscience, but shouts in our pains: it is his megaphone to rouse a deaf world."[42]

When a sudden tragedy occurs, many who otherwise don't give God a passing thought search for divine comfort. Others shake their fists at God. Either way, during the onslaught of our greatest trials, many people somehow sense He exists.

Because of the extreme capability pain holds to stimulate much-needed growth in our lives, it may be the most powerful force God can use to crush our misconceptions. Unlike any other stimulus, pain helps us remove the masks of our superficiality. As our disguises disappear, we become more capable of looking in the mirror and seeing our true selves more clearly.

For those with hardened hearts, great grief may be the only stimulus capable of breaking through the thick crust formed by our preconceptions. When self-help or the assistance from family, friends, and even experts fail, divine comfort stands alone offering solace during times of great uncertainty. This naturally occurring phenomenon between our needs and God's ability to supply comes rooted in the relationship between who He is and what He made man to be.

Explanations from the Scriptures

The Scriptures are full of explanations reflecting the role pain plays in the life of a believer. The entire book of Job is an example. For the purpose of our discussion, I've chosen a few shorter passages to highlight what I was learning. Writing in the first century after Jesus' death to Jews who followed Jesus, the New Testament writer, James, introduces his audience to the critically important role pain played in their lives:

> "Consider it pure joy, my brothers and sisters, whenever you face trials of many kinds, because you know that the testing of your faith develops perseverance. Let perseverance finish its work so that you may be mature and complete, not lacking anything."
>
> (JAMES 1:2-4)

What James teaches opposes our instincts. We naturally avoid pain. If we could choose, all our situations would be pain free. In fact, we make many of our plans by considering the risks of whether disasters could occur. But against our natural inclinations we are told that perseverance through adverse circumstances plays a significant role in bringing about our ultimate well-being. After listing the extreme difficulties he experienced since becoming a follower of Jesus, Paul explained the purpose pain played in his life:

> "I have worked much harder, been in prison more frequently, been flogged more severely, and then exposed to death again and again. Five times I received from the Jews the forty lashes minus one. Three times I was beaten with rods, once I was pelted with stones, three times I was shipwrecked, I spent a night and a day in the open sea, I have been constantly on the move. I have been in danger from rivers, in danger from bandits, in danger from my fellow Jews, in danger from Gentiles; in danger in the city, in danger in the country, in danger at sea; and in danger from false believers. I have labored and toiled and have often gone without sleep; I have known hunger and thirst and have often gone without food; I have been cold and naked."
>
> (2 CORINTHIANS 11:23-27)

Despite being surrounded with various difficulties at every turn of life, Paul explained how he carried an additional unshakable pain wherever he went. He surmised that the surpassing revelations God gave him could be a source of boasting. God chose him, against all others, to be the ever so sharp tip on His spear. But Paul's hardships prevented any arrogance; they kept him humble and reliant on God to see him through every step of life:

> "To keep me from becoming conceited because of these surpassingly great revelations, there was given me a thorn in my flesh, a messenger of Satan, to torment me. Three times I pleaded with the Lord about this, that it should leave me. But he said to me, 'My grace is sufficient for you, for my power is made perfect in weakness.' Therefore I will boast all the more gladly of my weaknesses, so that Christ's power may rest on me. For the sake of Christ, then, I am content with weaknesses, insults, hardships, persecutions, and calamities. For when I am weak, then I am strong."
>
> (2 CORINTHIANS 12:7-10 ESV)

I also considered the story of Joseph and how he was sold into slavery by his jealous brothers. Through his mistreatment, Joseph grew from a spoiled child to a man of great wisdom and humility. Many years after Joseph's separation from his family, the pharaoh in Egypt put him in charge of the Egyptian kingdom. Joseph and his family reunited when his brothers came to Egypt looking for food during a famine. Responding to his brothers' plea for forgiveness, Joseph said to them:

> "'Do not be afraid, for am I in God's place? As for you, you meant evil against me, but God meant it for good in order to bring about this present result, to preserve many people alive. So therefore, do not be afraid; I will provide for you and your little ones.' So he comforted them and spoke kindly to them."
>
> (GENESIS 50:19-21 NASB).

Good from evil—sounds antithetical at first. However, as we've seen, our most difficult moments provide us the opportunity to see more clearly how God works to offer us our ultimate good.

The Mystery of Unanswered Questions

In the end, I determined that those who demand pat answers for why tragedies proliferate in our world will be disappointed. I found that no matter how much you and I search, many questions concerning the mysteries of pain will go unanswered. Like so many other aspects of our lives, comprehensive explanations lie beyond our reach. Our limited perspective doesn't allow us to understand or make sense of everything.

Some who place themselves in the "great thinker" category declare humans to be entitled to a full explanation.[43] Skeptics claim that if their minds can't grasp how our current situation makes sense, then no explanation is possible. Because they view pain as inconsistent with the notion of a loving God, they conclude that He must not exist. But I discovered that the truth stands against these conclusions. Further, those who make these assertions and conjure up arbitrary rules for how to test for explanations regarding our pain remove themselves from the possibility of finding true understanding.

It made sense to me that if we're created beings, we shouldn't think that our Creator is obligated to tell us everything. The Scriptures indicate that God created the world in precisely the manner He wanted (Genesis 1–4). There were no divine mistakes or accidents. Therefore, because God chose not to provide a more complete explanation, it's possible that the balance between what we're able to know and what we don't know is to our advantage. A more complete explanation could undercut the potential benefit God's process was designed to provide. In other words, to tell us more could work against what God wants to accomplish in our lives.

The mysteries associated with pain highlight how God's ways are above and beyond our understanding.

> "For my thoughts are not your thoughts,
> neither are your ways my ways," declares the LORD.
> "As the heavens are higher than the earth,
> so are my ways higher than your ways
> and my thoughts than your thoughts."
>
> (ISAIAH 55:8-9)

Pascal once wrote that God gives us the light we need to find Him but at the same time He also doesn't overwhelm us, blinding us by any light.[44] Therefore, if God is real, all powerful, loving, and intimately involved in the details of each life, the pains we experience are both allowed and for our ultimate benefit.

Pondering these things I began to think of this issue from God's perspective for a moment. The Scriptures say that God the Father wants to give His children everything. He gave us Jesus, His beloved Son, who offered Himself entirely for each of us. In the end, Jesus' painful death, and all it represented provided the way for us to return to Him and be with Him forever. If the agony suffered by Jesus was necessary to usher in the salvation of mankind, we should certainly hold out the possibility that the pains that besiege us could be part of a process that provides a benefit for our individual lives.

My New Understanding About Pain

Therefore, based on what I discovered, I came to some new conclusions about the topic of pain. First, whether experienced by a skeptic or a follower of God, in the same way fire reshapes the Sequoias' forest environment, pain clears out the accumulated debris stimulating growth in our lives. By collapsing the foundations of prejudice that impair our judgment, a sudden injection of pain enhances the ability of truth to reach the fertile soil of our souls.

Secondly, when we experience the greatest pains in life, our stale thinking suffers the heaviest and most pulverizing blows. Grief pushes us to look to the inmost portions of our being and entertain questions not often pondered. Although pain is not something anyone desires, it holds the power, maybe unlike any other force, to refresh and clear out our dull thinking.

Thirdly, the pains we experience don't preclude the notion of God. The Scriptures say that God detests the unnatural conditions resulting from the separation between Him and His children. He desires to comfort us with the vision of how wonderfully He made us and how He plans to reverse the downward cycle of our self-destruction. One of the tools He uses to offer us the seeds of true life is the experience we encounter in the depth of life.

God's greatest hope is that the fire of our pain will refine us. He wants to transform us from our self-imposed, poor, ragged, and dirty condition to what He calls us to be. Learning to seek and depend on God, relying on His comfort, while working through the pains we experience in this life are vital parts of our development.

So, if we interpret intense, permitted suffering according to the Scriptures, we will not view those circumstances as solely destructive in nature. Rather, we will view the fire of pain as an unprecedented opportunity to receive the truth God offers, which is that He loves us so much more than we can comprehend. Or perhaps, we will come to grips with the reality of God and His love for the very first time. We might also grasp how this valuable instrument in the hands of a loving Creator could bring about our *ultimate* good.

The Beckoning

I acquired a newfound energy and purpose in life after marrying my wife Nichole and adopting our three beautiful children: Cody, Connor, and Grace. Pouring my emotional energies into my family became my new life. Nichole and I gushed with pride as I guided our relatives through the courthouse to the final adoption hearing for Grace, our third child. Little did we know, weeks later, our hearts would shatter like never before. Our precious son Connor died without warning, just a few months before his fourth birthday.

I can say categorically that no force of any kind ever hit me with such devastating fury. Suddenly, in the midst of hemorrhaging tears, my heart cracked open like never before. Months gave way to years. In my broken state, I ached for my son. In a new way, I was yet again living out Jesus' declaration that, "In this world you will have trouble" (John 16:33).

In vain I cried out that I'd give anything under my control if I could only put my cheek against his again. It took a long time for me to understand that no matter how much love we shared, my son wouldn't want to return to this life. He wants me to join him in the new life he's now experiencing.

During this most difficult time, I was reminded of how even Jesus in the moments before He was betrayed struggled with the prospect of the intense pain that lay before Him. At the precipice of Jesus' final hours, He asked the Father whether he could finish His work on earth another way. The answer indicated there was none.

It's no different for you and me. We may plead to be freed from the circumstances that cause great grief. We may develop elaborate strategies to shield us from disasters. However, as a result of the sum of all mankind's disobediences, which you and I continue to add many of our own, we will inevitably suffer the effects of living in this corrupted environment. To that we have no choice. We do, however, maintain the power to decide whether we will reap the beneficial side of our difficulties by seeking the Comforter throughout those circumstances, as well as beyond.

Think It Through! Talk It Over!

1. How has pain caused you to reflect on the meaning of life?
2. Why do you agree or disagree that pain can be beneficial?
3. Do you think most people would seldom pray if they never experienced pain? Explain your answer.
4. What might Satan tempt you to say or do if you were struggling with pain?
5. Why do you agree or disagree that Jesus sympathizes with human suffering?
6. Why might a good person suffer pain, while an evil person seems to avoid pain?
7. What do you consider to be the worst kind of pain: physical, emotional, mental, or spiritual? Explain.
8. How would you answer the question, Why does a loving God allow natural disasters?
9. Why do you agree or disagree with the claim that the rewards of faith are health, wealth, and success?
10. Has pain refined your character? If so, how?

Chapter 7

GOD'S MESSENGER: THE BODY

"For just as each of us has one body with many members,
and these members do not all have the same function,
so in Christ we, though many, form one body."

ROMANS 12:4-5

To view Michael's introductory video for Chapter 7,
please go to www.michaelminot.com/thebeckoning

ike most atheists, I relied on a few core arguments to substantiate my views. First, I knew of no reason to believe in a Creator because everything we see can be explained by science. As do most atheists, I also found it impossible to reconcile the everyday pain that's all around us with the concept of a loving, creator God. So, when I began my investigation, I was particularly interested in discovering how the Scriptures attempted to explain these topics.

But what persuaded me the most and caused me to be most fervent about my views was the hypocrisy of many leaders in the church. The shocking behavior displayed by some of these high profile Christians fueled my atheism. In fact, what I observed in these situations bears more responsibility than anything else for choking off my interest in investigating the Scriptures.

The first of these events that served to solidify my atheistic views occurred when I heard the news that former Methodist pastor, Rev. Jim Jones, had poisoned more than 900 people on his agricultural compound. Some of those who died were children and infants. Over the next few months, I became both angered and frightened as the media continued to offer details of this horrific incident. How could something as massive and disastrous as this happen? I began to wonder when the next Jonestown-type incident was going to occur? I also questioned whether people like Jim Jones were living near me and attended any of the churches in my community?

Later, in the early 1980s, the era of televangelism began when evangelists started buying airtime on television. The two preachers with the most airtime both ended up in sex scandals. After profuse apologies, one continued his preaching on television. A short time later he was caught with a prostitute. The other was indicted on accounting fraud charges and served time in prison for embezzling millions of dollars from donations.

Needless to say, these events made a significant impact on my thinking. They became the building blocks that erected a large, thick wall in my mind. Whatever philosophy these guys were pushing, I didn't want to have anything to do with. I wanted to stay as far away from them and their followers as possible. As nice and pleasant as people could be on the outside, what I heard in the news about these men developed a strong suspicion in me that anyone calling themselves a "Christian" might be hiding something sinister.

For these reasons, I knew at the beginning of my investigation that I'd have a great degree of difficulty being unbiased.

Scripture Tells It Like It Is

A short time after I began reading the Scriptures I encountered something unexpected. Rather than calm my fears about Christian leaders, what I read initially only served to heighten them. I know that no one's perfect. Every human has faults. But I didn't anticipate that so many dramatic examples of human imperfection would come from an unlikely group— Scripture writers.

One of the most passionate Old Testament authors was King David, who lived a thousand years before Jesus. David was known for his nobility, generosity, and forgiveness. Yet few stories of human failure paint a more tragic picture than that of David's life. He reached his lowest point in life in the events surrounding his illicit relationship with Bathsheba, the wife of a trusted servant who was away at war. After learning that his mistress was pregnant, David sent for her husband, hoping that he might be intimate with Bathsheba and thereby conceal David's identity as the child's father. But his scheme failed. In a second desperate attempt to cover up his despicable deeds, David sent his truehearted servant back to the front lines. Loyal to the end, and oblivious of David's plot, the faithful soldier died in battle serving his king. David then married his pregnant adulteress, an act that threw his entire kingdom into turmoil.

The life of James, Jesus' younger brother represents another prominent example of enormous misjudgment. Among Jesus' many younger siblings, James was the oldest brother. Arguably, no one knew Jesus better than James. But when Jesus announced He was God's Son, James not only ended their relationship but also heckled Him in public.

Jesus expressed His deep disappointment with James when he commented, "A prophet is not without honor except in his own town, among his relatives and in his own home" (Mark 6:4). Not until Jesus' death and post-resurrection appearance did James, with great humility, renounce his disbelief in favor of a newfound love for his brother.

Then there's Peter. No survey of imperfect Scripture writers would be complete without mentioning him. He was the first disciple to proclaim Jesus as the foretold Jewish Messiah. Referring to Peter as a rock, Jesus asserted that His followers would at some point be organized around Peter's faithfulness, stability, and leadership skills (Matthew 16:18-19). But Peter's many professions of love and dedication for Jesus didn't preclude him from later denying to strangers that he even knew Jesus.

Another unlikely Scripture writer appeared on the scene after Jesus' death. Paul became a powerful spokesperson for the resurrection of Jesus to the Jews, Greeks, and early Christians. With compelling logic, he authored at least thirteen inspired letters that today make up a substantial portion of the New Testament. But the period of time in Paul's life when he proclaimed Jesus as Lord stands in sharp contrast to the view he once held.

As a young devout Jew, Paul became incensed with the fact that some people were proclaiming that Jesus had risen from the dead. Consumed with conviction and loyalty to the religious leaders, he obtained permission from the high priest to arrest and prosecute any of those blasphemers he could find. However, while zealously pursuing his bloodthirsty campaign against Jesus' followers, he awakened to the fact that his understanding of Jesus was entirely wrong. Suddenly, he realized how his vicious crusade had set into motion the imprisonment, torture, and even killing of innocent men, women, and children. His victims were the ones who understood and lived the truth. In a few short moments, Paul came face-to-face with the weight of *his own heresy.*

To my surprise, I discovered that the writers of Scripture were far from perfect yet God chose them despite their many failures. David's repentant heart and zeal for God caused the Lord to refer to him "as a man after God's own heart." Similarly, James became one of the most influential leaders in the early church as the head of its Council in Jerusalem. As Jesus predicted, Peter became the "rock" of the early church. And Paul became the most influential Christian missionary of the first century—and probably of all time.

Chinks in a Skeptic's Armor

As I mentioned in chapter 1, my friend, who challenged me to investigate the Scriptures also suggested I visit a church located about twenty-five miles from where I lived to hear a pastor named Peter Lord speak. This invitation made me even more uncomfortable than my friend's challenge to read the Scriptures. My greatest apprehension was based on the fact that I didn't know whether hypocrites like those in the news I mentioned earlier attended this particular church. Thoughts of being lulled into some dangerous or sinister scheme filled my mind as I considered my friend's request.

A few weeks after I started my investigation, just as I had accepted my friend's challenge to read the Scriptures, I decided to attend a service at the church he recommended. I wanted to be able to say I was genuinely trying to investigate Christianity's claims. One Sunday, I found myself seated off the center aisle at Park Avenue Baptist Church in Titusville, Florida. I knew nothing about this church or its pastor. But then again, I didn't know much about any church. Whether Lutheran, Nazarene, Pentecostal, Baptist, Methodist, or any other denomination, they were all places I'd never been before. My expectation was that I'd get my attendance card punched and report back the obvious—that the experience didn't interest me.

After someone I presumed to be a pastor invited everyone to greet those seated nearby, a music leader led the congregation through numerous songs. To my utmost surprise, I found the experience startlingly beautiful. People all around me expressed themselves as if they were experiencing the highlight of their week. I barely noticed the song leader's singing and background accompaniment over the hundreds of distinct voices echoing through the building.

I wasn't accustomed to hearing harmonized singing accented by low volume accompaniment. Having attended more than fifty hard rock concerts, my prior music experiences featured amplified decibel levels that simulated a Category Five Hurricane blowing out a candle. And I was the candle. This experience, however, was peaceful, soothing, and inspiring.

After the final song, the person my friend spoke about gave a sermon that was both enlightening and practical. What struck me most, however, was what happened during the moments he spoke directly to God, rather than the congregation. In what appeared to be a display of awe and reverence for God, everyone gave their full attention to the moment. No one in the building moved. Everyone and everything was quiet and still outside the speaker's voice. I wondered whether hundreds of people were all simultaneously holding their breath. The manner and words of the speaker, along with the response of those around me, caused these minutes to be most thought provoking.

By the end of his talk, I assessed the speaker to be a highly intelligent man, appearing to be authoritative on the subject of the sermon, yet humble and kind. From all indications, the speaker garnered great respect from the audience.

I was forced to take notice of all I saw and heard.

At the conclusion of the service, some headed for the parking lots. But considering that a substantial number of people stayed, my curiosity compelled me to linger. Why were these people not leaving? I came to realize they used the time after church to visit with one another.

Considering my great desire for social activity, this was my first observation at the church to which I immediately connected. But even so, this was different from my social experiences. People huddled in groups all over the building. The degree of joy they expressed was unusual. Only in family reunion settings had I observed interaction like this before. But these people could not all be family. And my guess was they saw one another often.

After arriving home and pondering the events of the previous few hours, I conceded my church visit didn't go as expected. As if this concession constituted an act of personal treason, I quickly reassured myself that my skepticism remained intact. But regardless of my self-assurances, I detected chinks in the thick armor of my unbelief. Unable to be wholly dismissive, I found myself wanting to better understand what lay behind all that I witnessed in this church.

Clearing My Mind of Bias

Shortly after my visit to the church I read the following Scripture:

> "See to it that no one takes you captive through hollow and deceptive philosophy, which depends on human tradition and the elemental spiritual forces of this world rather than on Christ."
>
> COLOSSIANS 2:8

I recognized as I read this verse that I was in essence "captive" to a certain philosophy. I mentioned earlier that there was appoint in time early in my investigation when I recognized how I didn't enter into this investigation free of significant bias. Reading this verse is what helped me recognize this fact.

I understood the verse was speaking more to a situation that was probably different from mine. However, the underlying point was well taken. I agreed that people should be clear minded and free from prejudice when making decisions about what we believe. We shouldn't follow others only to run off the cliff like lemmings.

I couldn't get the portions of the verse that were challenging me and my prejudice out of my mind. For days I thought about the situation while driving, grocery shopping, or doing almost anything else. My pondering about the verse ultimately resulted in one of the most significant decisions of my life. I resolved to not be captive to anything. Every part of my thinking as well as the information that came from my reading would be put to the test. Every assertion must stand on its own merits. On other matters, my assumptions had been proven wrong before. Therefore, I determined that I should be open to that possibility regarding my philosophy too.

I also determined that no matter how much apprehension I held concerning the leaders of the church, I came to what I later would view as one of the landmark decisions in my life. I decided that no one's actions can either create or discredit the truth about whether God exists. God exists or doesn't independently of the actions of any person.

As a result, I now was able to position myself as a juror willing to go wherever the evidence led.

A second turning point soon followed.

The Blinders Came Off

My initial thoughts were that the writers of Scripture resembled the people I was reading about in the news. But I learned how those writers became great in God's kingdom not by being perfect—or even close to perfect. Regardless of their catastrophic blunders, they chose to accept the forgiveness God offered that would set them free from their selfishness, fears, and misunderstandings. God chose these flawed individuals to author portions of Scripture after their monumental mistakes, not before.

I found out how none of the Scripture writers, nor anyone else who ever lived, can claim to be flawless. The Scriptures indicate that "all fall short" (Romans 3:23). Feeling like one of David's slingshot rocks hit me between the eyes, I was stunned to read how God's forgiveness is available to all no matter their past. One verse written by Paul I had to read again and again, "For it is by grace that you've been saved, through faith—and this not from yourselves, it is the gift of God—not by works, so that no one can boast" (Ephesians 2:8-9). I'm not sure why those words were so difficult for me to understand. At one point, however, the blinders came off. A significant part of the story line of the Scriptures now made sense like never before.

Armed with this information I could better answer questions that before I couldn't begin to answer. "What is the church?" for example. I could now understand that the church, or the "Body" as it's referred to in the Scriptures, is a collection of people like the second criminal on the cross who asked for and accepted the forgiveness Jesus is so willing to give. I also came to understand that not only is no one perfect but no one becomes perfect by asking God for forgiveness. They're simply forgiven.

The failures of the men I mentioned and all others who've followed them set up an interesting paradox. For reasons I didn't fully understand, God chooses to reveal many of His attributes through an unlikely source—the testimony of men and women. God sees fit to tell portions of His great love story for man through the misadventures of highly imperfect mortals. And this isn't limited to the Scripture writers. It appears He's using anyone willing to be used in this way each day.

C.S. Lewis in his famous book *Mere Christianity* describes the situation this way:

"He [Jesus] works on us in all sorts of ways: ... through Nature, through our own bodies, through books, sometimes through experiences which seem (at the time) anti-Christian.... But above all, He works on us through each other.

"Men are mirrors, or 'carriers' of Christ to other men. Sometimes unconscious carriers."[45]

With my prejudices neutralized and my blindness corrected, I began learning a tremendous amount about the Body.

What I Uncovered

I concluded from my studies that the church I visited represents a small part of something much bigger. In its most accurate sense, a church is not a physical structure made of bricks and mortar. Nor is its central purpose to function as a social club, perform rituals, or act as a bloc of social activists. Each local group is part of a universal, worldwide family of God's followers.

I determined that the people in the larger Body of followers are drawn together and strengthened by a complex mix of factors. First of all, the church communities of today trace their origin back to a common beginning. After His resurrection and before He departed Earth, Jesus directed His followers to, "go and make disciples of all nations, baptizing them in the name of the Father and of the Son, and of the Holy Spirit, teaching them to obey everything I have commanded you" (Matthew 28:19-20). Shortly after this instruction, the apostles started speaking with a boldness and passion they never had before. They began telling all who'd listen of Jesus' resurrection and the hope they could receive by believing in Him.

On the first of those occasions, Peter spoke with unshakable confidence to a large crowd in Jerusalem, "and about three thousand were added to their number that day" (Acts 2:41). Days later, Peter spoke again. This time, "the number of men who believed grew to about five thousand" (Acts 4:4). These vibrant responses to Peter's first messages began a mighty chain reaction that would reverberate around the globe to the present day.

Within days, thousands of transformed men and women began serving as carriers taking the truths of Peter's message wherever they traveled. As a result, Christianity began spreading rapidly with pockets of new believers springing up in almost every direction. In response to receiving the truth, believers started gathering in groups to celebrate their relationships with God. While together, they nourished their newfound faith by reading the sacred writings and discussing the apostles' teaching.

Many new followers were poor, but they had become spiritually rich. Overflowing with thankfulness, they didn't need to fully understand the reason for a commandment before they obeyed it. Instead, they trusted that each of God's instructions was designed to move them to their best spiritual condition. Totally absorbed in the interests of the heavenly kingdom, they spoke openly of their faith, unconcerned with whatever personal consequences they might suffer if others misunderstood them.

What a Fellowship!

What attracted people to the bright flame of this revolutionary attitude the most, however, was not the boldness of Jesus' followers. Instead, what caught their attention more than anything was the deep love and commitment believers displayed for one another. Without compulsion, they formed informal help groups—mutual aid societies—within their communities. Every follower considered the pain of others his own pain. The Book of Acts describes this phenomenon:

> "They devoted themselves to the apostles' teaching and
> to fellowship, to the breaking of bread and to prayer.
> Everyone was filled with awe at the many wonders

and signs performed by the apostles. All the believers were together and had everything in common. They sold property and possessions to give to anyone who had need. Every day they continued to meet together in the temple courts. They broke bread in their homes and ate together with glad and sincere hearts, praising God and enjoying the favor of all the people. And the Lord added to their number daily those who were being saved."

(ACTS 2:42-47)

As I read about the early followers, I got the sense that no one among them was destitute. It seemed that those in need received their basic necessities from the others. As Tertullian, one of the first-century church leaders explained, "One in mind and soul, we do not hesitate to share our earthly goods with one another. All things are common among us but our wives." [46] But the outside world became even more amazed at another aspect of this giving attitude. In a way unlike the rest of society, these people cared not only for their family and friends but for those they didn't even know. Living out Jesus' teaching to love others as themselves they reached out to help widows, orphans, the sick and the poor the best they could.

These first actions of the Body represent the common beginning for all of today's Bible-believing churches.

A Tapestry of Spiritual Gifts

Ironically, another reason I found that caused Jesus' followers to fit together so well is because of their *differences*. From the time of Jesus till now, people of widely varying backgrounds, from every race and every nation, have come together to praise Him. Without respect to age, language, educational background, or net worth, the Body celebrates how God makes each person unique. Take yourself, for example. No one has ever held the same blend of talents God instilled in you, not even one of the apostles. You're a perfect example of how God distributes uncommon combinations of spiritual gifts among different individuals.

God designed each of us with different abilities so we can fill each other's gaps. In the case of God's followers, by bonding together, they offer their distinguishing and various gifts for the common good of the Body. In this way, each person within this rich diversity contributes to meeting the needs of others.

Similar to how material for clothing is made by crossing and interlacing threads, a garment of help for each other is fashioned from the unique individuals longing for God. Each believer represents a specifically placed, interwoven living fiber stitched into the quilt of the Body. Have you ever seen what happens when a thread is missing or hanging loose from a piece of clothing? Once a thread is missing, the others begin to weaken. Similar to how each thread in a garment supports and helps hold the others together, every believer is vital to the Body.

The apostle Paul put it another way. Drawing an analogy from how the various parts of the human body work, in His letter to the Romans he tells us:

"For just as each of us has one body with many members, and these members do not all have the same function, so in Christ we, though many, form one body, and each member belongs to all the others."
(Romans 12:4-5)[47]

I found from my investigation of the Scriptures that loving God and being loved by Him will never be a solitary affair. Each follower can only experience his or her highest, most unspeakable joy by setting aside a stand-alone attitude in favor of all being part of the whole. What happens when a falling raindrop meets the surface of a pond? It immediately becomes part of the pond! Similarly, when a person becomes a follower of Jesus, the Scriptures indicate that it's only natural for her to join in and operate within a common group. By joining the Body, she affords herself the opportunity to achieve heights of human fulfillment unknown to the solitary person.

The Body's Strength

I also discovered how an additional part of the Body's strength comes from how its members become nourished by the same source of truth. Shortly after Jesus' death, a few apostles and some other disciples began traveling the eastern side of the Roman Empire. Their sole purpose was to pass on the details of Jesus' teaching, His love for them, and the fact of His resurrection. They taught from the same Scriptures Jesus taught. To assist in spreading their message, some chronicled Jesus' life in manuscripts we refer to as the Gospels. These first-century missionaries also sent letters to further help people understand the truth given them by Jesus. Collectively, these manuscripts and letters are known as the New Testament.

Today, people in the Body worldwide read these same texts. The Scriptures supply all God's followers with identical truths. As a tuning fork establishes a standard tone for musical instruments, the words of these sacred writings serve as a common authority for the faith and conduct of all believers. Through the teaching of Scripture, God's followers maintain an uncanny ability to live with amazing similarity regardless of time or location. Their lives march to the beat of the same music throughout the world and throughout each generation.

The Body is also fortified by how God permits His life to simultaneously be enjoyed by every disciple. Regardless of location, no follower can be at any time beyond God's presence. "Surely I am with you always, to the very end of the age," Jesus promised (Matthew 28:20). This common, universal access to the same source of life refreshes, sustains, and inspires all the members of the Body in like fashion.

Difficulties In the Body

But despite making these discoveries about the Body, a number of questions remained: In light of God's abundant provision to His followers, how can we account for the many failings found within the Body? Why does our Christian friend or neighbor act in ways that sometimes hurts others? What causes some church leaders to fall into the very traps they warn others against? Why do you and I do things we later regret?

As I read more deeply in the Bible, I discovered the unfortunate reality highlighted by these questions results from a number of factors. The first difficulty within the Body is that a person's foolishness and selfishness do not vanish completely after he or she becomes a believer. Scripture describes God's followers as displaying sheep-like behavior. Sheep, as you may know, are easily led astray (Isaiah 53:6 and Psalm 100:3). Sheep don't take care of themselves. More than any other class of livestock, they require endless oversight and meticulous care. No wonder Jesus said that, "I am the good shepherd; . . . I lay down my life for my sheep" (John 10:14-15). We need that much attention! But still, many tend to wander from the lush pastures to which our Good Shepherd leads us. Far too often, followers stray away from Him into barren fields to gnaw on weeds and dirt. Commenting on our flawed condition, Charles Colson writes:

"In reality, the church is a messy thing. It's an organic body made up of strange and broken people—dirty sinners who need to be cleansed, sweaty soldiers who need to be equipped for spiritual warfare. The church is not a club for perfect people; it's imperfect, sometimes unpredictable, a cross-section of life, and the Holy Spirit uses it to draw lost sheep home to the Father." [48]

Secondly, as we'll see more specifically in chapter 10, Satan seeks to bring about the demise of everyone who follows Jesus. Again, the animal world exemplifies Satan's strategy. Wolves attempt to scatter sheep by separating vulnerable individuals from the protection of the herd and shepherd. Unfortunately, as every sheep rancher knows, sheep scatter easily. Once detached from the group, individual sheep are easy prey. Similar to wolves, Satan seeks first to deceive and then to destroy God's followers by enticing them away from the protections afforded by the Body. Exploiting whatever bitter or resentful attitudes believers may harbor, Satan attempts to drive believers back to solitary living and a selfish demeanor. "Only there will you be safe from the risk of love's hurts," he whispers.

The Perpetual Relay of Truth

By the end of my investigation, I began to see how, in spite of many blemishes, the church provides a visual representation of an invisible Savior. The Body does not issue its principal challenge to others by conducting Sunday services, performing rituals, or promoting moral behavior. True believers do not define themselves by a set of rules dictating how they should act. Rather, the church exemplifies the One who supplies them true life by demonstrating His love. How they treat their family members, their colleagues at work, and spend their time and money reflects how they cherish their relationship with God.

In his book *Being The Body*, Charles Colson tells us that:

"As America and its allies wage war on terrorism, our nations have powerful tools at hand: elite special forces, sophisticated weaponry, economic sanctions, massive electronic intelligence, armies, navies, and air forces on alert. These are the tools of war in the kingdom of this world.

"But in the kingdom of God, the tools are different. We are armed with faith, hope, truth, love, and the good that overcomes evil. It's a great paradox: Bearing these weapons that seem so weak, the church is the one institution in society that can provide strong moral resolve and spiritual inspiration that feeds the soul, cares for the needy, and guides those who have lost their way. It is the church that creates the character that will carry us through the historic struggle of our times. It is the church that will endure forever, even as the kingdoms of this world topple and fall."[49]

Often the world ignores what believers say. But when God's followers link arms with others on the same journey and model His love, observers face a more compelling reason to take up their quest for truth. Genuine love displayed by believers encourages others to unlock their prejudices unlike anything else.

I began to see from what I was reading that true believers don't seek attention for themselves. Instead, just as an accomplished dancer draws our attention to the beauty of the dance, not the dancer, belief in action points to the Creator, not the believer. God first invests His truth in the lives of those who love Him. Then, God's disciples pass along this passionate reality by loving others and mentoring those coming to faith.

I read many accounts of how reflecting this light cost some dearly in worldly terms. Throughout history, many ran a rugged path to pass the torch of God's truths to the next generation. These men and women sacrificed much to see something accomplished far bigger than themselves.

Many endured being shunned by their families and cast out from their communities. Some suffered physical torture, imprisonment, and even martyrdom. Though millions have been mercilessly persecuted and continued to face persecution for nothing more than their faith, the light of God's truth continues to shine as a result of their loving efforts. Occupying all periods of time, this relay of truth runs from generation to generation.

The Beckoning

Prior to conducting my personal search for the truth, neither I, nor anyone else could've imagined that I'd become a participant in this relay. *Anyone but Mike!* some said. The decisions I made following my journey caught not only me but also everyone who knew me by surprise.

What began as an attempt to preserve a friendship turned into a season of turning points. My journey started with my examination of the Scriptures, an examination of science, and a visit to a church where I witnessed the singing, teaching, and most of all, the genuineness of others. The sum of these experiences implanted a curiosity in me that prompted further exploration.

Soon, the underlying truth supporting the faith held by those I witnessed in the church became known to me. Over a period of months, my eyes began to see, for the first time, the fundamental truth of what it means to possess true life. Without being distorted by a host of personal prejudices, the radical fact of my creation and the infinite love of my Creator laid bare before me. Unable to ignore all I learned, I embraced what it means to truly and authentically be me.

After accepting these realizations, I completely reoriented my life toward seeking the One who supplied my very life. No decision, before or since, made as much sense or brought me such abundant joy. Not only did I accept God and His love for me, I desired to learn how to return His love as completely as possible. For that reason, and for the joy of being His, I told God that I wanted to say "yes" to anything He asked me to do. Writing this book is one of my responses to what I perceive He's asked me to do.

And so, as I look back, I see the paradox of God using imperfect mortals, such as the Scripture writers, as His messengers. Even today this pattern continues. I know this because this writer, arguably one of the most arrogant, proud, and self-righteous among men, has become one of them.

Think It Through! Talk It Over!

1. Have you been adversely effected by religious hypocrisy? If so, how?

2. What evidence of genuine Christian faith and practice have you observed? Has what you observed helped you overcome the hypocrisy you witnessed? If so, how?

3. Why do you agree or disagree that being forgiven doesn't render a person perfect?

4. How do you explain the apostles' boldness to proclaim the gospel?

5. Why do you agree or disagree that bias blinds many atheists to the fact that God exists?

6. How do you account for the flaws you see in some Christians' character and conduct?

7. Why do you think God included the failings of notable believers in the Bible?

8. Fill in the blank. The Church today is too _____ for its own good. Why did you choose the word you wrote in the blank?

9. What examples of genuine love have you seen Christians display?

10. How would you define "Christian fellowship"?

Chapter 8

GOD'S MESSENGER: OUR CONSCIOUSNESS

"So God created mankind in his own image . . ."

GENESIS 1:26

To view Michael's introductory video for Chapter 8,
please go to www.michaelminot.com/thebeckoning

One of the questions I'm asked most often is whether there were any issues I wasn't able to fully reconcile with my atheistic worldview. My answer is always, "yes." There was one issue that acted like a pebble in my shoe. It irritated me because I had no satisfactory explanation.

I was reminded of this fact recently when I saw an online post from a young lady. This is what she wrote:

> "Have you ever just looked at someone and thought,
> 'holy _ _ _ _, i really love you'?
> They're just talking
> or humming
> or watching a movie
> or reading a book
> or laughing or something.
> There's something about them in that moment—
> their body is alive
> there's a light in their eyes,
> something that makes you think 'i just really love you.'
> it's a weird sensation to think this,
> but it's pretty awesome that we can feel this way
> about another human being.'"[50]

These words, particularly the last three lines, remind me of a desire I've had since childhood, to understand the emotional aspects of our lives.

Loving and Learning

My mom and I had a wonderful time together when I was a toddler. She was a stay-at-home mom, and I was her first born. My early childhood was filled with wonderful memories of Mom pouring herself into me. We took trips to the park and the beach. We enjoyed piggyback rides and always shared lots of laughter and great fun. Then, suddenly, a challenge came to my idyllic world in the form of my first day of Kindergarten.

As with most children who've spent the first five years of their lives at home, I feared anything that threatened to take me away from the only life I knew. Afraid of being separated from my mom for such a long period of time each day and how that might jeopardize our intense love for each other, I protested passionately. Regardless, I arrived at school on that first day feeling heartbroken.

Though my first few days were rocky at best, my fears subsided quickly. Soon, I was making friends and enjoying the learning process. I remember coming home a month or so later and thinking, "*Wow, I really liked Kindergarten.*" I had enjoyed so many new experiences and met many new friends. Similar to the young female poet, I began wondering how I was able to feel this way. Where did all these emotions come from?

My mom would later describe me as constantly wanting to understand things to the best of my young mind's ability. Never surprised by my questions, she always tried her best to supply the answers. However, when I asked her how I could feel this intense love for her and also have feelings for others, she couldn't give me a complete answer. She simply admitted, "It's a mystery."

I don't recall thinking much more about this mystery until late high school when emotions are super charged and often dominate a teenager's life. My curiosity about the nature of love surfaced again but this time on a deeper, more adult level. Where does this wonderful ability to love come from? How does it happen? I also wondered about the origin of my creativity, reasoning skills, and my sense of what's right and wrong. I even wondered where the ability to ponder such things came from.

Avoiding My Doubts

While in college, I asked a number of people to help me with my questions concerning the origin of human thought and our ability to love. The explanations I received were all based on the theory of human evolution. People told me that once the process of biological changes reached a certain level of improvement, specific configurations of evolved matter could produce the thoughts and emotions that play such a big part in our lives. I knew when I heard these explanations that those who believed in evolution, such as myself, depended on this type of reasoning for all their arguments. If Darwinism is true, everything we see and experience, including what takes place in our mind and emotions, is made possible by the process of gradual changes to life forms over time.

But none of these explanations made sense to me when it came to what takes place in our mind. Even though I appreciated the efforts of those who defended evolution, I wasn't able to accept what they were telling me. It didn't seem probable that the process of biological evolution alone could adequately explain the complexities of our thoughts, our ability to learn, or our emotions. The perspective that the theory of evolution explained all this seemed too shallow. Both intuitively and intellectually it didn't make sense. How could human thought, emotion, and self-consciousness emerge from mindless, accidental, natural processes? How could something that's material produce something that's immaterial?

From a philosophical standpoint, I agreed with what most atheists say about how the pursuit of money, fame, and recreation are what give us purpose and happiness in this world. I based my schooling and first few years of my professional life on this view with one notable exception. I believed that more than anything else, my relationships with others made my life worth living. Certainly, the quality of my life and my mental well-being were enhanced when I experienced and developed healthy relationships. I knew my innermost qualities, the ones that gave me the ability to have relationships, were just as much a part of who I was as my physical body.

Truth is Important

I've always thought of myself as someone who loves to discover truth. During my class studies I came to appreciate my encounters with new truths, seeing what I'd never seen before. As a result, I've tried not to position myself against what I found to be indisputably accurate. For this reason, I felt stymied. Each time I pondered how we're able to love, learn, remember, dream, feel anxious, etc., I had no good answers; none that were intellectually satisfying. I couldn't reconcile why I had all these capabilities that played such a dominant role in my life.

As an atheist, this is where I felt most vulnerable. So, despite my desire to know and live by the truth, I decided to avoid thinking about it. But I didn't avoid experiencing the full range of emotions that come from enjoying relationships with other people and loving them deeply. Figuratively, I put this entire issue in a box that I titled, "The Unexplainable." Unfortunately, I became comfortable with this approach. Looking back, this was my head-in-the-sand way of avoiding the truth about my origin.

Looking to Science for Answers

Once I started my investigation I wanted to take a more responsible approach and dig into these matters more thoroughly. I first turned to the area of science. I was reminded of the methods physicians use to determine what's taking place with respect to our bodies. People in the medical field use machines to get a reading of our blood pressure; a thermometer to check our temperature; and a stethoscope to check our heartbeat. They may order blood tests, urine tests, a battery of X-rays, and an echocardiogram, among a host of other diagnostic procedures. Though helpful in many ways, none of these tests reveal what we're thinking or what's taking place regarding our emotional well-being.

The reason tests on our body don't reveal what's taking place in our consciousness is because our thoughts and emotions are separate from our physical make-up. Professionals are trained to find out more about our emotions and thought-life by administering personality tests, conducting interviews, and by studying our behaviors. But the extent to which we allow them to peek inside is largely under our control.

Here's a personal illustration. My father used to enjoy playing a game with me he called "Twenty Questions." The object of the game was for me to determine through investigative questions what my father was thinking. He would first tell me the general category of his thoughts. For example, he might tell me that he saw someone I knew, or observed something interesting, or maybe tell me what he observed, but I had to guess where the incident happened. I had twenty opportunities to ask questions that my father would answer with either a "yes" or a "no." Nothing about my father's physical body gave me any clues as to what was in his mind. Even if I had the opportunity to test my father's body using professional equipment, the results wouldn't have helped me succeed at the game. I was forced to use questions that probed his mind and he needed to respond.

My Investigation of Consciousness

We rarely think about the fact that we're made up of two distinctive parts. Separate from our physical or biological functions, professionals categorize everything that occurs inside us as our consciousness. Another way to think about it is that our consciousness is what we lose when we go to sleep.

Most of us take for granted how upon waking each morning our mind immediately re-engages so we can resume the process of being aware of ourselves and our surroundings. While we sleep, our consciousness and the emotional aspects of who we are lie dormant even though our body continues to function. But when we awake, our consciousness automatically reengages with our environment. Once again, we're able to make sense of our surroundings as well as express ourselves to others. Without having to flip a switch or push a button, our consciousness begins assessing what's taking place around us. All we have to do is wake up!

In large part who we are, our self-identity, is determined by how we choose to process what's going on around us. We may use our bodies to *express* ourselves to each other, but the most fundamental part of who we are is something other than the sum of our physical parts.

As an example of how your consciousness functions, at this very moment your consciousness is hard at work helping you evaluate the concepts I offer in this book. Processing new information, comparing and contrasting it with existing thoughts, and then generating new, more detailed views is something you do every waking moment. But that's not all. At the same time, your emotions are also constantly reacting to everything your five senses are detecting.

Our consciousness enables us to experience beauty, meaning, purpose, and other joys as well as anger, frustration, and fear. It helps us build relationships prompting us to seek out the company of others. Some argue that our emotions help keep us alive. An example is when fear helps us to be cautious and elude danger causing us move swiftly when needed.

Without our emotions life would seem pointless. We wouldn't do or accomplish much. But because of our emotions, we can look out and imagine the possibilities of what might lie ahead. Simply said, our emotions are the single most important factor why we experience such a meaningful, dynamic life.

The Philosophy of the Mind

As part of my investigation I also learned how people in the past have speculated about what makes human consciousness possible. Traceable back to the time before Plato, I came to know how our mental functions and their relationship to the body have been debated at great length. This wide-ranging subject has more recently been referred to as the "Philosophy of the Mind."

I learned how scientists have been trying for hundreds of years to discover the location of our consciousness. But despite their extraordinary efforts, and using extremely sophisticated technical equipment, they've been unsuccessful. Most scientists, psychiatrists, and philosophers admit they have no idea how our consciousness works. From a scientific viewpoint, the issue of the origin of our emotions and other parts of our consciousness remains an inexplicable mystery. Just like my mom said!

Daniel Dennet, one of the most outspoken and prominent atheist philosophers of our generation, explains his perspective on the situation this way:

"A mystery is a phenomenon that people don't know how to think about—yet. There have been other great mysteries: the mystery of the origin of the universe, the mystery of life and reproduction, the mystery of the design to be found in nature, the mysteries of time, space, and gravity. These were not just areas of scientific ignorance, but of utter bafflement and wonder. We do not yet have all the answers to any of the questions of cosmology and particle physics, molecular genetics and evolutionary theory, but we do know how to think about them. With consciousness, however, we are still in a terrible muddle. Consciousness stands alone today as a topic that often leaves even the most sophisticated thinkers tongue-tied and confused...."[51]

Mr. Dennett's candid statement illustrates the difficult reality all atheists face. Our consciousness is so complicated that it eludes explanation. The issue is made even more difficult considering that our consciousness is what lies at the heart of each one of us. The issue is not one we can view at a distance like something we see through a telescope and then walk away from. Our mental and emotional processes go wherever we go. They're central to what gives us the ability to function and navigate through life. They're the most essential parts of what makes us human.

For these reasons, I found it ironic that the activities we engage in everyday, the experiences that touch our lives as we navigate through life and how we feel about other people, are matters that we have no way of adequately defining or explaining. I also determined that for atheist philosophers to concede they have no explanation for what's at the heart of who we are as human beings renders their explanation of our lives woefully incomplete.

What the Scriptures Say About Consciousness

In the early days of my investigation I was confronted with what the Scriptures say about our consciousness. They, too, described us as having two distinct though integrated parts to our being. Our body represents the physical side. It functions like a tent, a temporary place to dwell. Our consciousness, referred to as our mind or soul, will continue on after death (2 Corinthians 5:1-10). Paul, in his letter to the Romans, referred to this dual aspect of our being when he wrote:

> "Therefore, I urge you, brothers and sisters, in view of God's mercy, to offer your **bodies** as a living sacrifice, holy and pleasing to God—this is your true and proper worship. Do not conform to the pattern of this world, but be transformed by the renewing of your **mind**."
> (ROMANS 12:1-2, emphasis mine)

Elsewhere, the Scriptures say:

"Do not be afraid of those who kill the *body* but cannot
kill the *soul*."

(MATTHEW 10:28, emphasis mine)

One of the most startling claims in Scripture indicates our
consciousness represents some of the same mental and emotional
attributes held by God. Apparently, God desired to fashion us in a way
that passes on to us many of His own attributes.

"Let us make mankind in our image, in our likeness"

(GENESIS 1:26)[52]

Have you ever come across something and almost instantly knew
that it was highly significant but because of the depth of its meaning you
didn't know how to process it. That's how I felt after I read this passage.
At first, I didn't have a clue what it meant to be created in God's image.
But later, after months of study, I came to understand what attributes
the Scriptures were referring to when they say that we reflect God in
certain ways. Here are some of those attributes:

Creativity

Although we're unable to create physical objects from nothing
as the Scriptures say God can, we have a propensity for inventing
things. This attribute gives us the ability to design and making
things. Buildings don't design or construct themselves. Neither do
machines. Instead, almost everything we use in our modern world,
from the cars we drive to the computers we operate, is the product of
human ingenuity.

When we're not inventing new products, we display our creativity in
a variety of other ways through the arts, literature, and music. Our song,
dance, paintings, sculpture, and poetry all represent gifts of individual

creative expression. Moreover, our capacity to think creatively is so powerful it continues to work when we're not awake. Even as we sleep, we express our imaginations in our dreams.

Logical Thinking

As wonderful as our creative talents may be, many scholars suggest that our inventive and artistic gifts are not as impressive as our ability to think logically. Since the days of the Greek Empire, many philosophers have praised our problem-solving skills as our greatest human attribute. Some have gone so far as to say that our reasoning[53] capabilities are "the spark of the divine within man."[54] The people making these claims base their views on the fact that our critical thinking skills are always working, helping us to evaluate everything we observe.

The Ability to Distinguish Right from Wrong

In addition to our creative talents and reasoning skills, you and I also come with an internal moral compass. Something in us—as inescapable as the body itself—alerts us to what's wrong and approves of what's right. Like a navigational instrument, this inner voice gives us the ability to judge our thoughts and actions. Despite how often we ignore our conscious, each of us continues to maintain the ability to know right from wrong and be naturally attracted to what's good and true. Pastor and spiritual philosopher, Timothy Keller, in his book *The Reason for God*, wrote:

"All human beings have moral feelings. We call it a conscience. When considering doing something that we feel would be wrong, we tend to refrain.[55]

"We all live as if it is better to seek peace instead of war, to tell the truth instead of lying, to care and nurture rather than to destroy. We believe that these choices are not pointless, that it matters which way we choose to live."[56]

Our Amazing Range of Emotions

One of the most analyzed, yet difficult to understand features we have in common with God is our amazing range of emotions.[57] Our emotions are so complex that our brightest scholars have been unable to categorize all of them. Though no one knows exactly how our emotions work, experts agree that our emotions are at the center of almost everything we think and do. Though important for so many reasons, the most prominent role our emotions play is how they stimulate us to seek and cherish relationships with others.

Our ability to feel, our capacity to express our feelings, the capability to choose between right and wrong, our ability to ponder the significance of ourselves and our environment, and our inborn awareness of how to be rational, personal, and moral beings, are all part of what the Scriptures claim is our God-given makeup. Because we're embedded with this package of divine-like qualities, we're set apart and distinguished from all other beings.[58]

The Most Significant Emotion

Of all these different qualities we hold, it's our emotions that have intrigued me the most. As I look around, it seems that the whole world is mesmerized by our ability to love and our desire to be loved. We sing about it, write about it, hope for it, and express it in all kinds of ways. Like me, it appears that almost everyone believes they're at their best when they care for others and express themselves in unselfish ways. Without the ability to love, we'd be nothing more than a variety of self-centered individuals.

But no matter what I learned about the different aspects of our consciousness, I kept coming back to the questions: "How can we do this?" "From where do our feelings of love and friendship originate?" "How is it that we can comprehend and express such intense emotion?"

When I thought about these types of questions I felt uneasy. Like me, almost every atheist believes that each one of us has the ability to love. No one can ignore the deep devotions we're capable of having for another person along with the unexplainable feelings that accompany love. It's all such a vital part of the human experience.

Nearly every adult has at some time told someone, "I love you!" But how could any of us say these words and mean it if, as I believed, we're nothing more than accidental beings? Why are so many ardent atheists resolutely faithful and committed to their spouses? And why are we constantly making plans to get together with other people? By nature, we're social beings. This undisputed fact led me to believe that there may be something deeper and better that explains what's behind our desire for relationships.

Some Conclusions about Our Consciousness

After studying the scientific, scriptural, and philosophical issues raised by our consciousness, I arrived at two conclusions: First, what lies within us provides more clues to the true nature of our being than any other source. Secondly, the essence of who we are is made up of what's in our character and our heart. Our bodies merely carry our more essential parts around allowing us to experience life as we go.

I also found it ironic considering the central role our consciousness plays in our lives that not many of us spend time pondering why we have all these abilities. It's something like the parts of our body that do things we never think about. Who reflects even occasionally upon the process of breathing and how we absorb oxygen into our body every minute of our life. Likewise, no one walks around thinking about what's taking place inside their beating heart. And what about all the other cells that are hard at work in our bodies? When's the last time you thought about what the cells in your liver were doing? Regardless of how infrequently we consider what's taking place with the involuntary functions of our body, they're all working together, performing brilliantly, in order to allow us to continue living. If any of them failed to perform, we'd be in immediate danger.

The same is true with respect to our consciousness. We seldom pause as we go about our lives to think about all the functions it performs. Between the time of my childhood and my investigation, I rarely questioned why we have all these abilities. But finally, when I took the time to carefully look into this topic, I sensed I was at the beginning of understanding the Scriptures and myself in an entirely new way.

The Beckoning

It wasn't until I was nearing the end of my investigation that I started to understand what the Scriptures said about our consciousness as well as the big picture represented by the Scriptures. After months of study I began to understand that the Scriptures weren't written to simply provide information. They weren't just recounting historical events to help illustrate certain points. Rather, their stories, poems, and teachings were all tied to a personal, emotional appeal from God. More than anything else, the Scriptures were speaking of engagements between God and us on an emotional level. And to make us capable of responding to the invitations offered by God who's described as the most highly emotional being, He caused us to be emotional beings as well.

Ultimately, after much digging and thought, I came to the conclusion that the explanation provided by the Scriptures offers the best rationale for why we're able to think, learn, and love. When I finally was able to hear what each of God's messengers were saying, for the first time I began to understand the meaning behind the scriptural assertion that we we're made "in the image of God." Suddenly, the overall story of the Scriptures became much clearer. It felt like I was viewing tiles being fitted into a beautiful mosaic.

A few chapters from now I'll be giving you the full story of what I discovered about God's great plan and the part our consciousness plays in it. But first, I need to finish laying the proper groundwork by addressing the issues of heaven and hell as well as discuss the spiritual enemies that plague us in this world.

Think It Through! Talk It Over!

1. Do you believe your personhood is more than just physical? If so, why?
2. What differences do you see between human beings and animals? What do these differences tell you?
3. When were you first conscious of the following emotions: love, hate, joy, sadness, anger, anxiety?
4. How would you define human intelligence?
5. How does human intelligence differ from that of animals?
6. What evidence of human creativity have you seen?
7. Why do you agree or disagree that human creativity can produce harmful devices?
8. What do you think is the greatest proof that humans have a spiritual nature as well as a body?
9. Why do you agree or disagree that it is wise to let conscience be your guide?

Chapter 9

GOD'S MESSENGER: THE TALE OF TWO ETERNAL CITIES

"Do not let your hearts be troubled.... My Father's house has many rooms; if that were not so, would I have told you that I am going there to prepare a place for you?"

JOHN 14:1-3

To view Michael's introductory video for Chapter 9, please go to www.michaelminot.com/thebeckoning

*J*n January 2011, my wife Nichole and I traveled to Xian, China to bring home our youngest son, Joshua. During our visit, we had the privilege of touring what some claim is one of the most important archaeological sites in the world. Thousands of clay sculptures known as the Terra-Cotta Army and the elaborate mausoleum they protect were built in the third century BC by Qin Shi Huang Di, the first Emperor of China. Shortly after taking the throne, Di commissioned a workforce of more than a half a million laborers to construct an army that would accompany him into the afterlife. This massive labor force worked for more than thirty years until he died.

But the whereabouts of the Emperor's tomb remained a mystery for 2,000 years. Finally, in 1974 officials discovered thousands of ancient life-size clay soldiers each with unique body positions and facial expressions. They were buried in a field just outside Xian. Accompanying the soldiers were clay horses, wooden chariots, weapons, and other military equipment. This discovery led the searchers to the Emperor's tomb inside a hill next to the field where the Terra-Cotta Army was buried.

After viewing the enormous number of artifacts at the site, it became clear to me that the Emperor was keenly aware of how death was pursuing him every moment. He knew that either by early tragedy or old age, each human body ceases to function within a few short years.

For me, the sudden deaths of my three friends, and later, my son, have been painful reminders of how short life can be. Even now, years later, the harsh truth of life's frailty continues to play out in my life. As I write this book, I am forced to observe the vicious, yet slow decline of my father as his once bright mind and strong body succumbs to the onslaught of Alzheimer's disease.

Though some consider it morbid to reflect upon the effects of death, first as a skeptic and then as a believer, I've found that many liberating truths can flow from considering the brief nature of our lives. Confronting this fact reminded me of how important it is to prioritize how I want to spend my remaining days on earth. But as I was nearing the end of my investigation, the issue of our mortality began to interest me for other reasons.

As I studied the topics we've looked at in this book, I occasionally came across passages that described the purpose our current life holds and the role it plays in God's great plan. The more of those passages I read, the more my curiosity was piqued as to what the Scriptures said about the next life. So, to understand what the Scriptures taught about eternity, I dedicated some time to researching this subject. Catching me by surprise, by the time I finished my research, I came to realize that I'd stumbled across yet another one of God's messengers.

Heaven's Gate

One of the first things I noticed from the Scriptures is that the afterlife begins immediately at death. While on the cross, Jesus assured one of the men being crucified with Him that He would pass immediately from this life into His presence.

> "One of the criminals who hung there hurled insults at him: 'Aren't you the Messiah? Save yourself and us!' But the other criminal rebuked him. 'Don't you fear God,' he said, 'since you are under the same sentence? We are punished justly, for we are getting what our deeds deserve. But this man has done nothing wrong.' Then he said, 'Jesus, remember me when you come into your kingdom. Jesus answered him, 'Truly I tell you, **today you will be with me in paradise.**"
>
> (LUKE 23:39-43, emphasis mine).

Also, on at least two occasions the apostle Paul expressed his desire to complete his time in this life so he would encounter what immediately awaited him in the next life. In a letter to his friends in Corinth he wrote:

"I ... would prefer to be away from the body and at home with the Lord."

(2 CORINTHIANS 5:8)

Similarly, to the members of the church in Philippi he wrote:

"If I am to go on living in the body, this will mean fruitful labor for me. Yet what shall I choose? I do not know! I am torn between the two: I desire to depart and be with Christ, which is better by far."

(PHILIPPIANS 1:22-23)

After reading these passages I began to wonder what parts of us survive death. We know the physical bodies of those who've passed from this life stay here. That's what cemeteries are for. We also know the deceased take none of their possessions with them. The Scriptures indicate, however, that the soul, spirit, and consciousness of each deceased believer begin a new adventure in heaven.

Working my way through airport security recently reminded me of what the Scriptures say happens at the end of this life. Since the 9/11 attacks, governments throughout the world undertake great efforts to discover what people attempt to smuggle onto airplanes. As I neared the security station, I heard the security personnel giving instructions for everyone to remove their shoes and all metal objects including jewelry. These items, along with the contents in passengers' pockets, were to be loaded into bins to be scanned. While their belongings passed through a scanning machine, each traveler walked through another screening device.

I couldn't help relating this experience to what the Scriptures claim occurs at the end of life. We take nothing with us. Everything in our pockets, our shoes, whatever remains in our bank accounts, the car, in brief, all of our possessions stay behind. And unlike airport security stations, we'll never be reunited with our possessions again. The same can be said for whatever status or lifestyle we acquired. It's all left behind. Whatever we've become as a result of the choices we made on earth passes, but nothing else does.

Since our body doesn't go with us into the spirit world, the next question that came to my mind was the kind of body we'll have after death? Again, what we know about this topic is far less than what we'd like to know. But we do know that in the afterlife, after the resurrection, every believer will have a body with similar attributes to that of Jesus' glorified body. The apostle Paul wrote:

> "But our citizenship is in heaven. And we eagerly await a Savior from there, the Lord Jesus Christ, who, by the power that enables him to bring everything under his control, will transform our lowly bodies *so that they will be like his glorious body.*"
> (PHILIPPIANS 3:20-21, emphasis mine)

The Reality of Heaven: Life Fulfilled

My overall sense from the Scriptures was that even those with great imaginations can't grasp the wonderful things God plans for those joining Him in heaven. In many places the Creator is described as too good for us to capture the full depth of His goodness. We're told that nothing completely prepares us for what awaits.

Pondering heaven's beauty, Billy Graham wrote:

> "Imagine some of the most beautiful places in the world. Switzerland when the sun breaks over the snowcapped peaks and spills onto the slopes filled with wildflowers. A crystal clear lake, nestled among pine trees. A beach with white sand and

the gentle lapping of warm Caribbean waters. A night in the desert west with one million stars against the velvet backdrop. An autumn day on a quiet road in New England. An easy chair, a good book, a cup of hot chocolate, and a glowing fire when the snow is falling at home.

"Heaven will be more than that, because it is our Father's house, and He is a God of beauty. The same hand that made the beauty of this world has a more beautiful place prepared for us."[59]

When I think about the process God must have undertaken to create this environment, it reminds me of the large task necessary to prepare for the Olympics. Because of the massive amount of architectural, engineering, and construction activities that are required to design and build the residential villages and the venues where the athletic competitions take place, site selection typically occurs six to eight years in advance. Finally, after all the construction activity is completed, tens of thousands of people arrive to participate in and view the many athletic competitions the construction activity was designed to host.

Similarly, Jesus indicated shortly before His death that He'd soon be leaving to prepare everything that's necessary to receive His followers into their eternal home. But like the final brushstroke on an exquisite work of art, heaven won't be complete until the end of the current age when believers from every generation come together. Only after this gathering occurs can the entire Body present itself to God as foretold by the Scriptures (Revelation 19). This union that takes place between God and His followers will birth a process of perpetual, joyous love. Moreover, those who experience this unspeakable joy will bask in the glory of knowing they will remain united to God and each other forever.

Once in heaven, the Scriptures indicate that the trials and tribulations of the former earthly life give way to an entirely new way of living. Our heavenly body will not be susceptible to breaking down, experiencing pain, or death (Revelation 21:4). There will be no need for doctors, nurses, or hospitals. Instead, our eagerness to learn, explore, and experience true life will be fueled by a body ever teaming with energy. Our renewed mind will be full of curiosity, vision, and vigor for new discoveries.

No longer will our senses be limited by the dimensions of height, width, depth, and time. All sensory powers will be retooled and supercharged. So too, God's divine brightness will illuminate physical features never before imagined (Revelation 22:1-5).

As a consequence of receiving these new abilities, residents of heaven will be ideally suited to experience the full essence of God's loving character. To their great delight, their new minds and bodies will be like sponges soaking in God's divine essence. Each disciple will experience an all-encompassing peace that will saturate every part of his or her being.

Heaven Intersects Our World

Before beginning my investigation, I somehow had the impression that Christians believed heaven was a far-away place. But the Scriptures I studied describe God and the activities of heaven as being so close that they intersect our lives. At first, when I read the passages that describe this condition, I couldn't understand how things could be this way. We can't see outside our own dimension. We can't perceive the activities of the spiritual world directly. But during my scientific research I learned that many physicists have detected additional dimensions surrounding us that we can't perceive. They insist that the extra dimensions are there even though we aren't aware of them. Like the ability of some animals to hear wavelengths we cannot, the fact that we fail to perceive the activities in the spiritual dimension doesn't mean it's not real, active, and all around us.

The details of what's taking place in these realms lay beyond our understanding. And because our current environment is so very different from what the Scriptures describe is taking place in the spiritual world, for now, we can only imagine what lies beyond. So, for a time, this unseen reality remains a mystery. But from the beginning of the Scriptures to the end I found passages that describe God's interactions in our affairs. They also document how God sends angels to help us negotiate the difficulty of our lives.

Although we're puzzled by how all this works now, the Scriptures encourage us to know that someday heaven and earth will come together. God's followers will soon live together and enjoy continuous, intimate interaction in a world made for our eternal happiness. During our current, temporary situation, however, God's followers maintain the assurance that God is closer than the air we breathe. He promises never to leave us.

The Reality of Hell

In addition to informing us about heaven, the Scriptures also indicate that a second dwelling place, known as hell, exists. Physically speaking, a chasm separates the two eternal cities preventing any crossover from hell to heaven or from heaven to hell (Luke 16:25). But apparently, their proximity is very close. So close, in fact, that at least in certain circumstances those living in hell have the ability to see into heaven and hear what's taking place there. How else could the rich man mentioned by Jesus in the following passage be able to call out to Abraham on heaven's side of the chasm?

> "The time came when the beggar [*named Lazarus*] died and the angels carried him to Abraham's side. The rich man also died and was buried. In Hades, where he was in torment, he looked up and saw Abraham far away,

with Lazarus by his side. So he called to him, 'Father Abraham, have pity on me and send Lazarus to dip the tip of his finger in water and cool my tongue, because I am in agony in this fire.'

"But Abraham replied, '... between us and you a great chasm has been set in place, so that those who want to go from here to you cannot, nor can anyone cross over from there to us.'"

(LUKE 16:22-26)

From the perspective of those in hell, heaven will produces an effect similar to a well-lit room. In the book of Revelation John wrote, "There will be no more night. They will not need the light of a lamp or the light of the sun, for the Lord God will give them light"[60] (Revelation 22:5). Considering this, people dwelling in heaven will not often notice anything taking place outside in the dark. But those on the edge of the wicked, gloomy areas are able to observe those celebrating in heaven's radiance. Gazing into the lighted area, they're relegated to witnessing those carrying on with their never-ending festive activities.

How hopeless will it be for those exiled to obscurity? While members of heaven continually create pleasant memories, the members of hell have nothing to celebrate. Hell, the eternal misery society, traps people in a joyless existence. Those attempting to escape their agony by fantasizing something delightful will wail in grief. For as soon as a pleasant thought enters their mind, they face the nightmarish reality that absolutely no hope exists for anything pleasurable. Each attempt to find respite from these never-ending anxieties accelerates the torment. For as fast as one can generate a pleasant thought, it growls back the cruel message: There's no escape from the eternal city defined by its incurable evil.

Jesus offered a disturbing picture of hell to the people of Jerusalem. To symbolize hell, He referred to an area located just outside the city's southern wall known to its citizens as the Valley of Hinnom. This place served as the city garbage dump. Most of the town's animal carcasses, filth, and sewage were dumped there. No one wanted to be near the overwhelming foul smell of rotting animal flesh and garbage. To attempt to control the putrefying nature of the valley, fires were often ignited. But even as the waste and methane burned, it produced a smoldering stench that blended with the other horrid odors rising from the waste.

Those not allowed in the city, such as lepers, lived in caves along this valley. Without other resources, some scavenged amongst the waste. Jesus indicated that in many ways the valley of Hinnom portrays characteristics of hell. People dwelling there will live in detestable circumstances outside of heaven. By symbolizing hell in this way, Jesus was offering the people a constant reminder everyone was familiar with that represented hell as a place no one wanted to be.

Heaven's Gate

As I look at our lives and read Scripture it seems that God designed our time on earth to be relatively short so we wouldn't have to wait long to enter into an entirely new way of life. Our current life is described in the Scripture as something like a fuse that sets off the beginning of something much bigger and more significant. Because of this, the Scriptures assert that one of life's greatest moments is its conclusion when death ushers those who love and follow God into a glorious eternity. The best that our current life offers represents just a foretaste of what will be experienced in the life to come. A place of eternal peace awaits that has none of earth's harmful features.

Jesus encouraged His followers to confidently anticipate this future when He said:

"Do not let your hearts be troubled. You believe in God; believe also in me. My Father's house has many rooms; if that were not so, would I have told you that I am going there to prepare a place for you? And if I go and prepare a place for you, I will come back and take you to be with me that you also may be where I am."

(JOHN 14:1-3)

By drawing our attention to the next life, it appeared to me that God was attempting to woo us from a perspective that's different from His other messengers. What God offers through the messengers we investigated in the previous chapters mostly address the circumstances we encounter in our current life. But it seems that God offers His description of what happens at the end of this life to draw our attention to His long-term plans for us in eternity.

The Beckoning: Death, the Greatest Day

From everything I read, I began to see why God, in the midst of our difficulties, offers us a beacon of hope by telling us certain things about heaven. Like a lighthouse beckoning ships in from the seas, the reality of eternity calls us home.

After becoming a believer I've come to better understand why the Scriptures warn us not to make the mistake of seeking heaven as a pleasurable destination or an alternative to hell. Breath-taking surroundings, pearly gates, and streets of gold may beautify the living conditions. But far more important is the fact that heaven represents the place where every believer who ever lived will exercise the privilege of coming together to join with their Creator. Though astonishingly attractive and pleasant as a living environment, heaven's primary purpose is to serve as the setting where unlimited, unending love will be displayed without end. These relationships represent the one true heavenly reward serving as the root from which all other benefits flow.

During our time on earth, as a believer gets to know God better, his love for Him increases. And as his love for Him increases, the call of the world to participate in the innumerable counterfeits to true love becomes fainter and less appealing. Although we receive significant glimpses of heaven while we're here on earth, we see dimly as though through a veil. However, at the end of this life, the veil obscuring our understanding will be lifted in dramatic fashion. The disciple will then be free from the earthly battles of pain, shame, sadness, bitterness, and loneliness. The believer's last breath forever separates his soul from being haunted by evil and suffering the harmful effects of this temporal life.

For these reasons, the greatest day in a disciple's life arrives when the last hour strikes. This is the time she's been waiting for, the time when she finally enters the everlasting arms of her Heavenly Father. And for the first time, she finds all her hopes and dreams realized.

Death signifies the end of the earthly journey. For God's followers, they are finally going to their true, eternal home with all the bliss the word "home" brings to mind. Seeing God clearly for the first time is beyond all words or imaginings. Having prepared daily for this moment, the final earthly breath ushers the disciple into this perfect moment of union, a moment that lasts forever.

Think It Through! Talk It Over!

1. What recent event has made you recognize how uncertain life is?

2. Why do you agree or disagree with the observation that time flies?

3. Does the thought of dying frighten you? Why or why not?

4. Why do you think God allows our earthly life to be so brief?

5. Why do you agree or disagree that the afterlife begins at the moment of death?
6. What are the first words that enter your mind when you hear the word "heaven."
7. Why will you be glad to have a body like Jesus' risen body someday?
8. What do you think Jesus will say to you when He welcomes you to heaven? What do you will say to Him when He welcomes you?
9. How does the reality of heaven help you cope with global turmoil and personal circumstances?

THE COUNTERFEIT MESSENGERS

"Be alert and of sober mind. Your enemy the devil
prowls around like a roaring lion looking for someone
to devour."

1 PETER 5:8

*To view Michael's introductory video for Chapter 10,
please go to www.michaelminot.com/thebeckoning*

s a practicing attorney for more than twenty years, I've gained
an insider's view on the methods some people use to try to
trick others. But I don't need to rely on my experiences as a lawyer to
recognize that we need to guard ourselves against those who seek to
mislead us.

Some deceivers have become so savvy that they've been able to fool even the institutions with the most sophisticated verification procedures. Here's an example of what I'm talking about: In February 1999, John Myatt, an artist, was sentenced to prison for "perhaps the most ingenious and damaging art con of the twentieth century."[61] Over a nine-year span, Myatt produced more than 200 forgeries of fine art that were sold through the auction houses of Christie's, Sotheby's and Phillips', as well as other reputable dealers in London, Paris, and New York. Police and art experts were shocked at the ability of Myatt and his partner John Drewe to authenticate forged masterpieces.

According to the New York Times, "Drewe had systematically infiltrated some of the most security-conscious art archives in the world," altering the records that helped identify the original masterpieces. In the same article, Glenn Lowry, director of the Museum of Modern Art in New York City is quoted as saying, "What distinguishes this case is how methodical Drewe was, and how well he understood the process of validation. His manipulation of the system is as interesting and troubling as the forgeries themselves."[62]

This massive scheme of deception within the prestigious world of classic art merely touches the surface of how sinister plots exploit innocent people every day. Society is plagued with those pretending to be someone or something they're not while looking for opportunities to pirate everything from apparel to music to even pieces of art.

During my investigation, I could see how acts of deception played a part in many of the stories told by the Scriptures. I struggled, however, to comprehend how the battle between God's messengers and those that opposed the truth played out from a spiritual perspective. Though I found many helpful authorities on the subject, the breakthrough I needed came when I read *The Screwtape Letters* by C.S. Lewis.[63] The angle offered by this powerful fictional story illustrated how the forces opposing the truth operate in ways I'd never considered before. Armed with this new insight, I was then able to go back and reread the Scriptures in a different light.

Similar to how professional criminals push their fraudulent schemes on the unwary, the Scriptures tell us that two primary sources, Satan and the world, attempt to challenge, diminish, and corrupt the information offered by God's messengers. In light of this, the Scriptures also speak to our need to be prepared to distinguish between what's real and what's fake. The apostle Paul implored members of one of the early churches to be wise and discerning, "no longer infants, tossed back and forth by the waves, and blown here and there by every wind of teaching and by the cunning and craftiness of people in their deceitful scheming" (Ephesians 4:14). Writing to another group, Paul encouraged them to "Examine everything carefully; hold fast to that which is good: abstain from every form of evil" (1 Thessalonians 5:21-22 NASB).

So, after first considering what God's many messengers are telling us, in this chapter we'll take a brief look at what I found concerning the forces attempting to counterfeit them.

Unveiling the Impersonator

According to the Scriptures, the need to discern what's real began when Satan launched his rebellion against God. This landmark event started a conflict between good and evil that's been raging ever since.

Lucifer, meaning, "star of the morning," was once one of the most beautiful angels (Isaiah 14:12). But when he initiated a crusade to overthrow God, he lost his lofty position when God banished him from heaven. In retaliation, Satan assumed the role of God's chief antagonist. Contrary to what he was originally created for, he now works against everything good and true.

Satan will do anything to try to destroy our relationship with God. He constantly tries to drive a wedge between us and our Creator in order to rob us of the joy, peace, and fulfillment God offers. Because he carries a great amount of hostility and hatred against us, he targets us as his enemy and endeavors to destroy our lives (1 Peter 5:8).

Pastor and former Chairman of the Dallas Theological Seminary, Chuck Swindoll summarizes the results of Satan's activities by saying:

> "He continually seeks to destroy us through his evil workings behind the scenes. Satan and his demons may be invisible most of the time, but they are *real.* They have personalities and wills, and are absolutely committed to trying to destroy God's people and ruin God's plan."[64]

The Scriptures describe all of Satan's efforts as focusing on one primary end: that humans reach a state of intimacy with *anything* other than their Creator. Satan's goal is to lure as many undiscerning souls as possible into the trap of his false promises. He entices us away from God, hoping we fail to recognize, or even care about, our true identity as created beings. Rather than pursuing the truth, he encourages us to preoccupy ourselves with whatever fulfills our selfish desires.

Fortunately, God gives us advice how to best navigate through the obstacles posed by Satan. First, we are told that we're up against a relentless foe. Satan is constantly stalking us (1 Peter 5:8). Secondly, we should also be aware of his schemes so we can be better prepared to protect ourselves (2 Corinthians 2:11; Ephesians 6:11). Here are a few of Satan's tactics I came across during my examination of the Scriptures.

Satan's Covert Nature

An essential element of Satan's overall strategy is to operate in secret. Just like humans who carry out fraudulent schemes, Satan knows that to be effective his fallen angels must disguise their true identity and intentions. Satan's efforts to lead us into self-destruction would be futile if his evil nature were unveiled. Consequently, he has become a master in the art of camouflage and impersonation. He sows seeds of ruin in our minds covertly, disguising everything he does.

To guard against detection, demons attempt to morph into any number of inoffensive disguises. For example, sometimes Satan works through the voices of people we look to for advice such as philosophers, political leaders, educators, scientists, or even those claiming to be experts in religion (1 Timothy 4:1-3). To this end, he often portrays himself as a spiritual physician offering cures for our afflictions.

But one of Satan's best Houdini tricks is to convince people he's nothing more than a concept conceived by the minds of others. He knows that those who believe he doesn't exist fail to perceive how essential it is to understand his destructive schemes. How can anyone recognize the need to "be sober minded" and "watchful" (1 Peter 5:8), if they don't believe what they should be looking out for exists?

A Few Specific Tactics

One of Satan's specific tactics is his attempt to get us to fear or mistrust God. He boldly invites people to curse God for their pains. He does everything in his power to make us think we cannot trust God. He suggests God is simply standing on the sidelines allowing heartbreak and disaster to wreak havoc in our lives.

Moreover, Satan also knows that addictions can leave us feeling hopeless and powerless, which is precisely how he wants us to feel. Therefore, he's constantly trying to introduce us to a smorgasbord of addictive, soul-destroying passions such as compulsive gambling, adultery, and a dependence on alcohol and drugs. One of his favorite ways to snare men is to lure them into pornography. He snares women by making them think they need to look like the emaciated models portrayed in airbrushed photographs. But these are merely a small sampling of the vices into which he lures people.

Satan's evil task of destroying us is made much easier when we're enslaved by these destructive behaviors. Satan sees his mission to destroy his victim as substantially complete when we become so focused on meeting the demands of our addiction that we fail to address our need to investigate the truth of our lives.

To further dull our consciences, Satan goes on to suggest that we create a competitive advantage for ourselves by cheating, lying, or stealing. When no one's looking and the risks of getting caught are low, he says, "Go ahead. Just do it. There's no shame. Everybody else does it. After all, it's only wrong if you get caught. And besides, you have a lot to lose if you don't." He encourages us to ignore any thought of the rightness or the consequences of our choices. Today, it's not hard to see the scars our society bears from these temptations. Dishonesty in the workplace and schools has risen to epidemic proportions.

Satan also understands that for any of his misinformation to be effective it must be subtly interwoven with what appears sensible. Without any rational basis, only those with deranged minds would be foolish enough to follow his deceptions. Therefore, to lure us away, Satan is constantly trying to conjure up perversions that appear to be both reasonable and attractive. He tries to bait us with anything we might deem sensible or of value in order to pull us or keep us away from God.

Our Past

The Scriptures go on to describe how to the extent we fall prey to Satan's deceptions, he then hits us with a more punishing assault. Stepping into the role of our accuser, this devious fiend wants us to believe that the logical consequences of our downfalls are inescapable. He is always reminding us of our ugly past. He relentlessly replays scenes from our past, hoping we conclude that there's no escape from what we've done.

Ultimately, Satan wants to destroy us by guiding us into the repetition of our past mistakes. Wanting us to think our redemption's not possible, he feeds us his standard lie: "No one can reverse the irreversible." "You can't participate in any loving relationship," he says, "especially with God. You don't deserve it!"

As for me personally, it's impossible to deny the enormous number of my offenses. Even when judged by worldly standards, I've amassed enough wrongdoing to create a multi-volume record book. But when I came to the end of my investigation, I found Paul's testimony and instruction to be two of my greatest weapons.

Paul was responsible for the false accusation, imprisonment, and torture of many innocent people before he became a believer. With his sordid past in mind, Paul wrote, "Forgetting what is behind and straining toward what is ahead, I press on toward the goal to win the prize for which God has called me heavenward in Christ Jesus. All of us, then, who are mature should take such a view of things" (Philippians 3:13-15). Rather than live a defeated life, Paul chose the comfort and security offered by Jesus' words: "if the Son sets you free, you will be free indeed" (John 8:36).

Attacks on God's Messengers

Once ensnared in one of his lies, Satan doesn't want us to be jarred or disturbed by anything that could free us. He prefers we remain a society of spiritual illiterates with blinded minds and paralyzed wills. Rather than be awakened to the reality of God's love and forgiveness, he wants us to continue our careless living. Therefore, he tries to silence the truth by waging a continuous assault against each of God's messengers. For example, He cheers for those who encourage others to believe we are nothing more than a random fusion of molecules. He knows he's gained significant progress in muting the voices of God's messengers if he convinces us that our origin was simply a haphazard event.

Satan also attacks the Scriptures by enticing us to doubt they're the absolute truth. He suggests that the Scriptures should be interpreted as nothing more than a book of ancient fables. Unless he achieves some level of success here, he knows all other seeds of corruption will struggle to take root.

Knowing the critical importance the Body holds in God's plan, our archenemy unleashes some of his most vicious rhetoric on believers. In his attempt to undermine the Body, he asserts the Church is comprised of gullible, simple-minded people. "Religion is a crutch for people who need one," he suggests. "Besides," he says. "religion can be dangerous. The attitudes held by these people generate much of the conflict in society. How many wars have been waged as a result of conflicted beliefs?"

Satan's Attack in Paradise

Satan doesn't limit himself to using his wicked tactics one at a time. He typically hits his victims with a well-orchestrated barrage. To see what this looks like, let's take a look at how he tempted Eve in the Garden of Eden.

Satan began his encounter with Eve by posing a question that he hoped would plant doubt in her mind: "Did God really say, 'You must not eat from the tree in the garden'?" (Genesis 3:1). He then tried to manipulate Eve into questioning whether God's prohibition for her and Adam was fair. After Eve mentioned what God told her the consequence would be if she or Adam ate the fruit from a particular tree, Satan attempted to contradict what God told her. "You will not certainly die," he said (Genesis 3:4). Then, insinuating that God was keeping important information from Eve, Satan remarked, "For God knows that when you eat from it your eyes will be opened, and you will be like God, knowing good and evil" (Genesis 1:5).

Satan's schemes worked. Eve did precisely what God had commanded her not to do. She ate the forbidden fruit.

This episode further reveals the fundamental sequences Satan typically employs. First, he offers contradictions and distortions of the truth that God and His messengers offer. And then he invites his victim to take action based on his perversions of the truth.

Man's Distorted Culture

In addition to his attacks against individuals, Satan also injects his false ideas into our entire society. One of those false ideas purports that we should get all we can now because there's no ultimate future. See if you recognize any of these slogans from the world of commercial advertising.

"Live it up!"

"Do it now!"

"Have it your way!"

"You only go around once in life, so grab all the gusto you can!"

"Just do it!"

"You deserve it."

As a result of Satan's work, the world applauds those who seek to increase the abundance of their material possessions. Our society supports the mentality that we should all crave more "stuff."

Likewise, we should be driven by a never-ending desire for accomplishment. Whether in business, politics, or sports, success is defined by outcome. "You play to win." Society encourages us to compete to be richer, better looking, sexier, more athletic, and famous. This philosophy of winning at all costs drives many to desire to rise above their neighbor—*not to serve him*. We have normalized "What's-in-it-for-me?" thinking.

Our culture heaps praise on those who've accomplished much. Those who rise to the top are considered experts in their field. The best of the best are lauded with awards such as the Nobel Prizes, Pulitzers, Academy Awards, and the Most Valuable Player (MVP) award of a Super Bowl or World Series.

While basking in the moment of recognition, the recipients of prestigious awards inevitably express how happy they are to have achieved success. But only weeks later, many acknowledge that they didn't gain the satisfaction they had hoped for. They concede that something big is still missing from their lives. In response, Satan wants them and the rest of us to believe that our feelings of emptiness will go away if we just keep trying. He entices us to keep on striving, always searching for something more from what the world offers. But in the process, people develop the routine of experiencing one unfulfilling experience after another.

As we might suppose, Satan's advice contrasts sharply with the admonitions God gives us in Scripture. "Do not love the world or anything in the world. If anyone loves the world, love for the Father is not in them. For everything in the world—the lust of the flesh, the lust of the eyes, and the pride of life—comes not from the Father but from the world. The world and its desires pass away, but whoever does the will of God lives forever" (1 John 2:15-17). Colossians 3:2 admonishes us: "Set your minds on things above, not on earthly things."

While reading about Satan's tactics, I began to sense the real tragedy the Scriptures were describing. People trying to draw satisfaction from the world tend to become distracted. By focusing on the pursuit of one passing pleasure after another, people forget to seek the answers to life's most important questions. They don't realize that their disappointment comes from the very path they're pursuing. By not looking in the right place for what satisfies, they stay perpetually dissatisfied. For the charms of the world affect people like saltwater. Once ingested, they dehydrate the soul from the very substance necessary to live a true life.

Family and Relationships

Satan is also well aware that our relationships provide many opportunities to receive God's message. Therefore, Satan persistently targets our relationships. In her book *The Power of a Praying Parent,* Stormie Omartian describes the situation this way:

"One of the things the enemy of our soul likes to do is get into the middle of God ordained relationships and cause them to misfire, miscommunicate, short-circuit, fracture, or disconnect. The more family can be splintered apart the weaker and more ineffectual they become and the more the enemy has control over their lives."[65]

The stakes for us, our relationships, and our families in these battles have never been higher. We live in a new age that's teeming with fresh, innovative communication systems. Modern technology via the Internet has dramatically increased the opportunity for people to communicate on every subject, including the truth of God's love for us. But Satan is also using these same communication systems to poison our minds. Not only do most homes have multiple computers but also we carry communication devices with us everywhere we go via our smart phones and tablets. Satan no longer needs to entice us to leave our homes to fall into the dark temptations of society. Instead, access to "the world" and everything it offers is only a few clicks or taps away, twenty-four hours a day.

Our homes are now intense battlefields with a variety of enticements waiting for us on our Internet browsers. The ease by which we can access pornography, gaming, gambling, and other activities in complete secrecy has opened the door for Satan to lure unsuspecting people into addictions that can completely consume and destroy their lives.

Many online games attempt to seize the minds of our precious children who long to feel socially accepted and powerful. The makers of video games are masters at designing simulation games that reward players with a sense of power and acceptance. But ever so subtly, as a player progresses to higher levels, sometimes characters emerge who engage in horrific violent acts, drug and alcohol use, offensive language, and stealing. Rapidly, one's home can be host to fictitious characters and their behaviors that would be abhorred in real life. More shockingly, some games give Satan a new canvas to glorify his occult activity by introducing the innocent minds of our younger generation to the dark rituals of satanic practices. Would we ever take our sons and daughters to witness executions or satanic rituals? Of course not, but they can view them in video games.

Satan, the Master of Bait

As I read about all that Satan does to deceive us, I recalled the strategies I use when I go fishing. Like most fishermen, I have my favorite spots, techniques, and lures. My artificial bait of choice is a silver spoon that is nothing more than a bent piece of colored metal with a treble hook at the end. It's designed to imitate an injured baitfish by fluttering erratically as I drag it through the water. Unfortunately for each fish I fool, when it attacks the lure, instead of taking a bite of a tasty breakfast, it wraps its mouth around a prickly deceptive trap.

My use of artificial bait with sharp hooks is similar to the process Satan uses when he's attempting to lure us into believing his counterfeit messages. He's been trying to hook humans and drag them into his dismal abyss for a long time. He knows where to go and how to use his perversions of the truth effectively. He methodically casts each of his alluring lies in front of us in an attempt to get us to bite. When we think we are biting into something good, we soon learn to our dismay that Satan has hooked us and brought great suffering into our lives.

God's Promises—Satan's Limitations

The good news, according to the passages I was reading, is that God made us with a much greater intelligence than any fish. The Scriptures indicate that along with our ability to reason, God has given us many other tools to fend off Satan and his schemes. Because Satan and the demonic creatures that assist him are spiritual rather than physical enemies, God has equipped us for spiritual warfare. Writing directly to believers, the apostle Paul outlined the special equipment God provides for this *spiritual* warfare.

"For our struggle is not against flesh and blood, but against the rulers, against the authorities, against the powers of this dark world and against the spiritual forces of evil in the heavenly realms. Therefore put on the full armor of God, so that when the day of evil comes, you may be able to stand your ground, and after you have done everything, to stand. Stand firm then, with the belt of truth buckled around your waist, with the breastplate of righteousness in place, and with your feet fitted with the readiness that comes from the gospel of peace. In addition to all this, take up the shield of faith, with which you can extinguish all the flaming arrows of the evil one. Take the helmet of salvation and the sword of the Spirit, which is the word of God."

(EPHESIANS 6:12-17)

Considering how Satan is constantly trying to work on us from all angles, Paul indicated that we should always be ready, putting on each piece of armor that God has provided.

In addition to the Scriptures' description of Satan as a relentless adversary, they tell us that God promises that none of Satan's attacks, no matter how vicious, will ever overcome us. He cannot overpower us. Paul emphasized this fact in his first letter to the Corinthians:

"No temptation has overtaken you except what is common to mankind. And God is faithful; he will not let you be tempted beyond what you can bear. But

when you are tempted, he will also provide a way out so
that you can endure it."

(1 CORINTHIANS 10:13)

Additionally, together with our intellect and the tools God's given
us, our greatest resource is God Himself. He promised that we would
never face any of our battles alone. He's with you and me always, never
leaving us. He assures us that, "When you pass through the waters, I will
be with you; and when you pass through the rivers, they will not sweep
over you. When you walk through the fire, you will not be burned; the
flames will not set you ablaze" (Isaiah 43:2). Thus, we don't have to rely
solely upon our own thinking or power to be successful. God is with us,
making sure that "no weapon that is formed against you will prosper"
(Isaiah 54:17 NASB).

It seemed to me from what I had read that Satan would go beyond
his mass-production of counterfeit propositions if he was able. He'd
like to reach in and strangle our hearts. But God restrains Satan from
entering the place of our consent. As the Book of Job makes clear, God
limits Satan's means, mobility and efforts. He keeps him in check at all
times. Even though our enemy is allowed to tempt us, we always hold
the power to refuse his temptations. And as we will see in the next two
chapters, God's plan is such that we can live victoriously with joy, hope,
and great fulfillment.

The Beckoning

After reading about the counterfeit messengers and why the world
we live in is so far from perfect, I continued to have a number of
unanswered questions. Not about the background of the counterfeit
messengers or how the Scriptures claim they operate. But questions that
center on a more fundamental issue: If God had the power to set up our

environment in any way He deemed fit, why would He provide Satan direct access to our lives?

As we saw in the previous chapter, the Scriptures indicate that those in heaven now live beyond Satan's reach. But why would anyone have to wait for heaven to be set free from his or her struggles with Satan? Wouldn't our lives be a lot easier and less painful if we lived right now where Satan couldn't influence us? Since God is all-powerful, why didn't He confine Satan ages ago to a place where he couldn't reach us? Considering the enormity of the universe, wouldn't it have been better to consign Satan to a place that didn't coincide with where we lived?

These questions lingered with me for a short time. But eventually, the epiphany that changed my life hit me. Suddenly, and unexpectedly, I began to comprehend how God's messengers are all cast members performing their respective parts in one coordinated universal plan. Even more amazing was the revelation that our interactions with the counterfeit messengers fit perfectly in God's master plan as well.

Think It Through! Talk It Over!

1. What deceptive practices have you learned about recently? Which one struck you as being the most shocking? Why was it so shocking?

2. Why do you agree or disagree that our culture is ripe for deception?

3. How might Satan disguise himself today in order to gain people's confidence?

4. What lies about God and/or the Bible do many people believe?

5. How does Satan use the following baits to lure unsuspecting people away from the Truth: pleasure, money, relationships, technology, and success?

6. How does the Lord enable us to triumph over Satan's schemes?

7. What advice would you give parents who want to help their children avoid Satan's schemes?

8. On a scale of 0 to 10, how successful have you been at resisting temptation? How might you improve your score?

9. Satan forfeited his lofty position because pride caused him to covet God's position. How have you seen pride topple someone from a lofty position?

10. How does it help you to know God limits Satan's means, mobility and efforts?

Chapter 11

GOD'S GREAT PLAN (PART 1)

"Many are the plans in a person's heart, but it is the
LORD'S PURPOSE THAT PREVAILS."

PROVERBS 19:21

To view Michael's introductory video for Chapter 11,
www.michaelminot.com/thebeckoning

Some years ago, I had the privilege of traveling to Rome, Italy. While there, I took in many of the touristy sites such as the Coliseum, the ancient city ruins, arches, and fountains. One of the last sites I visited was the Vatican. Our tour began in St. Peter's Cathedral, the most magnificent church structure in the world. We then proceeded through a number of smaller buildings that housed many of the church's paintings, historical papal garments, and other artifacts. But nothing in all of Rome prepared me for what I saw at the end of the tour when I entered the famed Sistine Chapel.

Immediately prior to entering the chapel, our tour guide provided a brief history of the Chapel and Michelangelo's work there. We were told that the goal of Michelangelo's project was to depict the relationship between God and man through some of the scenes described in the book of Genesis. The research, preliminary sketches, and actual time spent painting the nine scenes on the ceiling took more than four years longer than it took to construct the building.

As our tour guide led us into the chapel, a reverent hush came over us. Whether stunned to the point of being unable to talk, or simply out of reverence, no one spoke. No one seemed able to do anything other than gaze upward in awe. A few minutes later, as we continued to try to absorb the elegance and majesty of it all, I noticed another group enter the room. With a quick glance, I could see they, too, were awestruck. It seemed like our responses were intuitively appropriate. After all, we were viewing one of history's greatest artistic achievements.

The Turning Point

To an even greater degree than when I viewed the masterpieces on the walls and ceiling of the Sistine Chapel, I found myself awestruck a number of times during the latter stages of my investigation. My first experience of this kind occurred when I began putting together what I learned from science. From our place in the cosmos to the incredible functions that take place within DNA molecules, the precision and numbers of interdependent relationships began to stagger my imagination. More and more, I recognized how so many essential elements are finely adjusted to make life on this planet possible. Constantly working together, they give us the just right living environment we need.

In the final analysis, I had to confess how unlikely it is that all of the conditions making our lives possible could be the result of random, unguided circumstances. There are simply too many conditions calibrated far too precisely to suggest an accidental origin. I had to admit it was far more likely that something intelligent played a part in making all this happen.

For entirely different reasons I found myself awestruck again a short time later while reading the final chapters of the book of Revelation. In very few instances can we know the future. But if I assumed for a moment that God was real, it appeared He was providing certain details of what's going to happen at the end of this age to help us understand the big picture of His plan. Knowing what happens in the end can sometimes help us put current events into proper perspective. In this case, that's what happened with me.

These final passages in the Bible describe a wonderful unity that's predicted to occur between God and those who'll be spending eternity with Him. In what I believe to be one of the most simple, yet informative verses, the Bible says:

> "Let us rejoice and be glad and give him glory! For the wedding of the Lamb has come, and his bride has made herself ready."
>
> (REVELATION 19:7)

From what I read, I came to understand that the "bride" in this ceremony is a large group of individuals made up of God's followers from every generation. The significance I placed on this event triggered many new insights that impacted my interpretation of most everything I'd read before.

Until this point in my studies, I viewed the Scriptures as a collection of ancient writings about various disconnected subjects.

But after reading how the final chapters of the Scriptures describe what's predicted to take place at the end, I experienced a turning point in my understanding. The joyous event I read about and all it symbolizes helped me better understand why so much of what we see around us is in the order we find it. It now appeared that everything I read in the Scriptures before these final chapters described God's efforts to prepare for this event and the age that will follow it.

From this revelation I began to see relationships, patterns, and an overall message emerge from the texts in ways I'd never seen before. I was better able to harmonize much of what I formally saw as fragmented pieces into a cohesive bigger picture. Suddenly I realized that the words in the Bible aren't offered merely to recount historical events or help illustrate a point. They're not just attempting to provide guidance as to a proper, moral way of living. And they're not merely attempting to provide evidence that we're created beings. Yes, I could see how they accomplish these things. But more importantly, I found that the Scriptures speak of opportunities to engage in relationships on an intensely personal and emotional level. When questioned, Jesus indicated that our ability to enter into deep relationships serves as the very reason we were created. Everything centers on loving God and each other.

> "Teacher, which is the greatest commandment in the Law?" Jesus replied: "'Love the Lord your God with all your heart and with all your soul and with all your mind.' This is the first and greatest commandment. And the second is like it: 'Love your neighbor as yourself.' All the Law and the Prophets hang on these two commandments."
>
> (MATTHEW 22:36-40)

All at once, the concepts of choice, our consciousness, our relationship to God, what God's messengers are saying, and even why God allows us to be influenced by counter messengers started to make more sense.

God's Harmonious Truth

With all this in mind, it made sense to me that everything we see and experience should fit into one cohesive pattern. If everything originated from one single source, we'd expect to find all the parts fitting together, working toward a common goal. Suddenly, my eyes were open to that possibility. Looking around, I began to see how God provides an abundance of clues evidencing His presence. He saturates His creation with many messengers who speak on His behalf, providing numerous opportunities for us to hear what He has to say.

I began to see how God uses the messengers we've investigated in this book to surround us with His voice. As we've seen, one of the ways we hear His voice is from what He's made. Inside the immensity of God's universe, the splendor of creation amazes us with its complexity and perfection. Our minds simply can't reach far enough to comprehend the magnitude of His incredible works. Only after passing from this life will we see with great satisfaction and admiration the distinct purpose each part held.

God made our physical environment with a perfect balance of influences so we can understand why we're here. Paul wrote in his letter to the Romans: "For since the creation of the world God's invisible qualities—His eternal power and divine nature—have been clearly seen, being understood from what has been made, so that people are without excuse" (Romans 1:20).

We also hear a significant portion of God's message through profound truths He reveals in Scripture. Unlike any other words we know, God's voice reaches into our hearts with explanations that describe the life He intended for us. His greatest desire is that we allow His words to help us comprehend life's purpose, His beauty, and our special qualities as beings made in His image. This single most important source of truth helps us interpret everything we see and experience.

In addition to nature and the Scriptures, we can know certain aspects of God's character by observing His followers. Although dispersed throughout the world, people from every background, race, size, shape, and sort gather to celebrate His love and to express their gratefulness for the gift of everlasting life. By their love and compassion for others, believers represent a bright light that shines against the backdrop of the world's spiritual darkness.

Even in our pain, we see God drawing people to the truth of their need for redemption. He uses our suffering as a tool to penetrate through our heart's outer crust. Then, He enlists our wounds into the service of changing us. In doing so, He's always drawing us closer to Himself.

Our reasoning capabilities, too, are also perfectly calibrated. We've been given just what we need to draw the proper conclusions from what we observe so that we may know God is the cause of everything, including our own existence.

After much thought, I came see how God utilizes diverse methods to voice different facets of His perfect plan. And much like Michelangelo's work in the Sistine Chapel, each of God's messengers seemed to fit into a beautiful masterpiece. Distinguishable, yet interrelated, these messengers comprise a communal articulation of the truth. Each messenger supplements, corroborates, and clarifies the others. Only the full range of influence given by God's messengers, with all of their provocative beauty and complexity, captures what God wants mankind to know.

We can say then that God, as the Architect and Source of all that nurtures us, illuminates the path to true life in many intricate ways. Without contradiction, everything surrounding us excites, invites, urges, and inspires us to see who we are as created beings. From the smallest particle, to the incomprehensible vastness of the universe, all things are structured so they fit together for our ultimate well-being. Each piece of God's creation plays its part to lure our affections to the divine privileges offered.

God, Man, and Redemption

In the midst of coming to grips with what I was learning from science and how God's messengers operate, I also faced another challenge. Before beginning my investigation, I listened to critics depict the God of the Scriptures as a demanding King, one that's impossible to please and quick to exact revenge. But once I perused the Scriptures for myself, I found Him to be totally different. The fact that God made us to be His children challenged the notion that He was cruel, revengeful, or uncaring. From what I was reading, I didn't perceive God as anything like a grumpy, old guy with a beard who's always ready to pounce on us.

The more I read, the clearer I could see from Scripture that "God is love."[66] Eventually, I recognized what nineteenth century spiritual philosopher George McDonald suggested when he wrote:

> "What is the deepest in God? His power? No, for power could not make Him what we mean when we say *God.* A being whose essence was only power would be such a negation of the divine that no righteous worship could be offered Him; his service would be only fear. The God Himself whom we love could not be righteous were he not something deeper and better still than we generally mean by the word *righteous.*
>
> "In one word, God is love.
>
> "Love is the deepest depth, the essence of His nature, at the root of all His being. Love is the heart and hand of his creation. It is his right to create, and his power to create.

It is out of His love that He *does* create. This perfection is His love. All His divine rights, His power, His justice, His righteousness, His mercy, His fatherhood—every divine attribute we think to ascribe to Him—rests upon His love. God's love is what He *is*."[67]

I also came to understand that God gave us the ability to love from His own nature. It's not hard to see, however, that we haven't exercised this ability very well. History demonstrates how we *continually* rebel against God. Instead of loving God back, we've developed many selfish tendencies along with a strong craving for earthly things. Some individuals have become so wrapped-up and self-identified with their particular style of disobedience as to fear they'll no longer be themselves if they abandon their rebellious attitude. Others, such as I was, have gone so far as to claim that God doesn't even exist.

But despite all our waywardness, the message the Gospels offer is that God gives us a chance to return to the place where we can enjoy a right relationship with Him, fulfilling the true purpose for which we are made.

What No One Explained to Me

These new revelations helped me understand why we have some of the key features we hold. If God wanted us to love Him, we must be equipped with everything necessary to exercise great love. With this in mind, God fashioned humans to be like Himself in many ways. He placed His divine imprint deep within, making each individual capable of knowing His voice and developing a personal relationship with Him.

I also came to understand how God knew that the love He seeks from us requires our free choice to actualize it. Only willing participants pouring themselves into each other are capable of reaching the highest levels of love. How could any meaningful relationship occur otherwise?

To say that a person can experience an involuntary or coerced love creates a contradiction of terms. For example, how can a young man and woman arranged to be married truly give their deepest feelings to each other on the first day they meet? A person might honor and respect someone out of obligation or duty, but authentic love with all its complexity and joys can't be imposed.

As the Creator, God had many options when deciding how much freedom to give us. First, He could have programmed us to respond like robots that would do and say whatever He wanted. The second possibility would provide us limited freedom like that illustrated in the arranged marriage example. But the more I thought about this issue, the more I appreciated why God rejected these options in favor of providing us the greatest amount of self-rule possible. He knew that anything less would severely limit the potential for any relationship He could have with us.

God's decision to give us our freedom didn't come without significant risk. By not forcing us to choose Him, we hold the power to reject Him. We can push God away and miss out on all He wants us to experience. But despite the risks, God knew He must give us the independence we need, the space within ourselves to debate and ultimately decide whether to come to Him.

To remove either our ability to choose, or the resulting consequences of our choices, would cost God all He hopes and works for. Rather, if the potential for great love is to remain possible, He must endure each of the circumstances flowing from the exercise of the human will.

Although I read many passages of Scripture emphasizing the significance of each individual's power to choose or reject God's appeal to respond positively to Him, here are two examples that drive home this truth. The first comes from Joshua's farewell address to Israel. Decades after leading the Israelites into Canaan, the Promised Land, and conquering the warlike tribes there, old General Joshua challenged the

Israelites to "choose for yourselves this day whom you will serve . . . . But as for me and my household, we will serve the Lord" (Joshua 24:15).

The second example derives from the final invitation Jesus extended in the Bible. He appealed to unbelievers to come to Him and receive "the free gift of the water of life (salvation)." "'Come!' And let the one who hears say, 'Come!' Let the one who is thirsty come; and let the one who wishes take the free gift of the water of life'" (Revelation 22:17).

So, after deciding to give us the most extensive power of choice possible, what does God do to persuade us to love Him? He beckons us in ways that speak directly to our liberty to choose. He sends many messengers that call us to Him. But no matter how many invitations God sends us or how influential they are, we can only be led, not dragged. In His deep desire for a relationship with us, God stops at nothing to gain our affection—nothing except coercion.

Think It Through! Talk It Over!

1. Have you experienced a turning point in your relationship with God? If so, what was it?

2. What examples of deception have you observed?

3. Why do you agree or disagree that God would never force anyone to believe on Him?

5. Do you think the freedom God gave human beings to love or reject Him leads you to love Him rather than reject Him?

6. What do you think is the most attractive feature of heaven? Explain!

7. If you had heard Joshua's challenge to choose this day whom you will serve, how would you have responded? Why that response?

8. What media slogans do you think fall in line with Satan's deceptive practices?

9. What characteristics of God have you seen reflected in His followers?

10. How does knowing "God is love" enhance your life?

Chapter 12

GOD'S GREAT PLAN (PART 2)

"'For I know the plans I have for you,' declares the
LORD, 'PLANS TO PROSPER YOU AND NOT TO HARM YOU,
PLANS TO GIVE YOU HOPE AND A FUTURE.'"
JEREMIAH 29:11

As I continued piecing the parts of God's great plan together, I knew I needed to address a few other topics that I had been using to support my atheism. The first, and possibly the most difficult issue was the problem of evil. As we know from our discussion in previous chapters, there's plenty that's imperfect in our world. Acknowledging this fact the Scriptures indicate, "We know that the whole creation has been groaning as in the pains of childbirth right up to the present time" (Romans 8:22).

But if everything fits together to accomplish God's purposes, how does our being subjected to Satan's wretched schemes fit in? In light of the power and authority God is described as having, He could've destroyed Satan or banished him to a faraway place. But instead, God gave Satan permission to enter the Garden of Eden to tempt Adam and Eve. He also permitted Satan limited access to us. But why would God do this? Why are we subjected to temptations like waves beating against the shore during a storm? To say that Satan's presence in our lives wasn't purposefully allowed would eliminate the notion that God is all knowing and all powerful. So, if the Scriptures are true, there must be an explanation why we find ourselves in such a vulnerable state.

I decided to approach the problem by asking: Could Satan's influence provide anything that might be considered a potential benefit to our lives? Or to put it another way: What would we miss if we weren't subjected to Satan's schemes? I eventually came across what I thought were three possible answers.

I found the first potential answer while studying the nature of relationships. If we were made in a way that gave us no option other than to follow God that would cause us, in effect, to be preprogrammed beings. As we previously discussed, without the ability to make meaningful decisions concerning our relationships, we wouldn't be able to love. Sterile environments where only right choices are available produce only sterile beings. And that's not the life God intended for us.

God made us to be His sons and daughters. He made us so that we could engage Him and each other at the highest, most profound levels possible. With this in mind, God arranged our circumstances so that we'd be free to make our own decisions from many alternatives. That way, our choices would be made in the most meaningful way possible.

So, for His good purposes and to ensure we have the conditions that are most advantageous to our ultimate well-being, God permits Satan to tempt us to a limited degree.

The Scriptures indicate that though Satan would relish the opportunity to reach in and strangle our hearts, he cannot overpower us as he would lead us to believe. Like all the other influences in our lives, the degree to which evil may make itself felt is restricted, measured, and kept in check by God.[68] God ensures that evil may only market itself to the extent necessary to facilitate our ability as free-will beings to choose between good (God's love) and evil (the absence of God).

The Scriptures also make clear that our temptations never originate with God. The apostle James wrote:

> "When tempted, no one should say, 'God is tempting me.' For God cannot be tempted by evil, nor does he tempt anyone; but each person is tempted when they are dragged away by their own evil desire and enticed."
> (JAMES 1:13-14)

A second possible reason I found for the existence of temptations and the evil around us is the fact that they challenge us. The effort we must exert to navigate through our struggles and rise above them leads us to a greater, more spiritually mature condition. The apostle James wrote:

> "Consider it pure joy, my brothers and sisters, whenever you face trials of many kinds, because you know that the testing of your faith produces perseverance. Let perseverance finish its work so that you may be mature and complete, not lacking anything."
> (JAMES 1:2-4)

Third, the necessity we have to respond to Satan's schemes provides both God and us the ongoing ability to test and measure the level of our spiritual condition. Moses reminded the Israelites that, "the LORD your God led you all the way in the desert these forty years, to humble you and to test you in order to know what was in your heart, whether or not you would keep his commands" (Deuteronomy 8:2).

From my time looking into all this, I could see how God provides His truth in a manner that stands more evident than Satan's misguided misinformation. But to prevail over this enemy, our selfish instincts, and the messages offered by the world, we must exercise the discernment God has given us. If carried out well, the challenges we face in life help us acquire a discriminating mind and a well-exercised, loving heart. And from what I read in the Scriptures, that's precisely why God puts us in this position. By exercising our judgment well we best prepare ourselves to engage in all that God has prepared for us.

God uses Satan as the primary instrument to offer us the alternatives we need. As antithetical as it may sound, God temporarily placed us in this broken world as a co-occupant with Satan, the father of lies, as part of God's plan of deliverance. We can say then that even the presence of fallen angels and their abilities to entice us is specifically prescribed. Like everything else, Satan, with his vast array of counterfeit offerings, unwittingly is a tool God uses to serve His purposes.

The Nature of the Divine Design

Another argument I used to support my views as a skeptic is that God wouldn't design anything less than a perfect creation. If, as the Christians claim, God is all powerful, all knowing, and all loving, wouldn't everything He created be free of imperfections? However, as we know, it's clear that weaknesses and imperfections do exist. For example, as I pointed out during my years as a skeptic, the human body has many conditions that I considered to be design flaws. Our eyes are a case in point. They produce blind spots and tend to scatter light. They also are susceptible to trauma, disease, and malfunction.

I've heard some scientists counter that each biological part is not designed to be individually perfect. Rather, each part is configured to maximize the best overall contribution to the organism. For example, having a pair of eyes, instead of only one, eliminates many blind spots. Other design factors accommodate the need for the eye to perform other functions, such as taking in oxygen.

I've learned, however, that the truth best supports a third position. As the details of the bigger picture started coming together, I began to realize that God's design goal when He created humans wasn't to produce the best physically functioning being. Rather, God set out to craft a living creation fashioned to receive all the benefits that come from being united with Him. To achieve this goal, God formed our temporary human bodies with *great* limitations. Think about it: we cannot run fast or fly at all. Many animals see much better than we do and others hear sounds in wavelengths we will never experience.

But despite our many limitations, God equipped us with every capability necessary to recognize what His messengers are telling us. We come perfectly suited to understand the spiritual significance of our lives and respond to God's invitations. Though no two of us are exactly identical, each of us has a mind, a body, and instincts that are ideally fashioned to recognize that God put everything around us into place. He never intended that we'd possess the most excellent biological functions. God designed us in a way that maximizes our ability to grasp His great love for us and make the choices He designed us to make.

Facing My Skeptical Attitude

To complete our discussion about God's great plan, I'll contrast a few more thoughts I held as an atheist with what I uncovered during my investigation. As a skeptic, I developed certain attitudes that had the effect of distancing me from the accountability of God's message. I used to say: "I have an opinion of the way an all-powerful Creator God should operate and because I don't find things to be that way, I won't believe in Him." You see, skeptics, like I was, often craft objections in a way that causes their self-created burdens of proof to never be met. As a result, they create barriers between themselves and the places they don't want to go. Here's an example of what I'm talking about.

One of the reasons I gave for my unbelief was our inability to understand all the details of heaven and hell. If God and His heaven existed, I found no reason why He should withhold from us the details of any afterlife. I also suggested that if a Creator existed, He'd let us see Him face-to-face and understand Him fully. Since we don't live in these conditions, I concluded that God must not exist.

One of the flaws in my theory was that I failed to recognize how God's plan is specifically designed to ensure that our responses to His messengers are genuine. As previously discussed, to make sure that His goals are accomplished, God established the degree to which all influences work in our lives. Even taken together, every means God uses to persuade us never reaches the point of overcoming our ability to make free choices. While always inspiring to the fullest extent, God never allows any situation to deprive us of our decision-making ability. He gives us everything we need to decide whether to accept His love for us, but He does so in a manner that powerfully provokes while not overwhelming us.

The underlying problem with my skeptical way of thinking was that I failed to accommodate the fact that certain truths have the power to be so persuasive that they create predictable responses. If all the details of the afterlife or what's currently taking place in the spiritual world were known, this disclosure would be so persuasive that almost everyone would become God's follower. The same is true if we were to see God face-to-face. This type of influence would surely overwhelm us. Therefore, if either of these conditions were to occur, it would have the effect of removing our freedom to choose to follow and love God.

As an atheist, I completely missed the critical nature of why God chose not to reveal all His plans and purposes. Our limited knowledge establishes the very condition necessary for God to ask us to trust Him. Trusting Him. Believing in Him. Following Him even when we don't understand. (See Proverbs 3:5). He wants our trust to be independent of acquiring a full understanding of things. God supplies us with innumerable answers to countless big questions. But, if we had *all* the answers to *every* question there'd be no need for trust. Because we don't have all the answers we're put in the position of needing to trust. And trust is what God wants us to have because it best matures the relationship He designed for us to have with Him.

As I came to understand more of what the Scriptures say about God's character and purposes, I also began to suspect how foolish I was to expect that God needed to explain everything. If God is real, I began to comprehend that as His creation, not His peer, I shouldn't expect He would inform me of every last detail. From what I read, it would seem that the full spectrum of God's motives were far too deep for my puny understanding to comprehend.

The Beckoning

Over the course of my investigation I admitted that some aspects of my worldview were being tested. Until the very end, however, I wasn't convinced there was enough evidence to draw me away from my atheistic beliefs. But after going over what I learned during the months I spent reading, analyzing, and pondering, a depth to the story materialized that I'd never seen before. Hundreds of fragments, both scientific and scriptural, now appeared as if they were brought together by a single synthesizing source. As the many pieces of information I reviewed merged into one picture I began to feel overwhelmed. Only then did I suspect I was entering into an entirely new dimension of understanding.

The early passages in Genesis indicated that God paused at the end of each of His "days" of creation and said that what He had made was "very good" (See Genesis 2). But these words beg the question, "Very good for what?" By the end of my investigation, I knew the answer. God had arranged every detail of the entire universe, including each specific part of our human makeup, in a way that would serve His purposes to both invite and draw us to our ultimate future. I could see how everything carries out its distinct design function. From the smallest parts to the vastness and size of the whole universe, not one single aspect was carelessly or unskillfully made. Every unique part was put in place after specific forethought as to its purpose and how it would fit in relation to the whole.

I found that I could no longer avoid the conclusion that our place in the universe and what we've been given are each tailor made for our benefit. The beauty and perfection of how the physical universe holds together; our inability to see God physically; and the separation between what the Scriptures tell us, and what they don't tell us, fits just right with our needs. God perfectly measured what we need in our heart, in our body, and in our exposure to surrounding conditions. Even the schemes of the enemy and the degree to which they touch our lives are all allowed for our benefit. All of these conditions link together to form the backdrop out of which we're drawn to the love of our Creator. Each of these many factors work to both enable and require us to decide whether to accept God's invitation to join in the most preeminent of all relationships.

In the end, I came to see that we live in a perfect setting, even if it doesn't always seem that way. Not desirous in any way as a permanent place to live, the experiences of this lower world are what's necessary to usher in what God wants for us at the end of this earthly experience. Only then will our deepest desires be satisfied. Until that time, we'll have to endure the enticements of the world and Satan's seductive temptations. But for those choosing to accept God's invitation, the first breath of heavenly air will mark the end of all their troubles. It is for this moment that we hope upon hope. Only after taking that breath will we begin to recognize the full measure of God's wisdom in everything He's done for us.

In this temporary life, true love sets our deepest, most wonderful emotions ablaze. This is the ultimate of all experiences. From an earthly standpoint, nothing else compares. Despite this, the most passionate human love represents merely a foretaste of the upcoming heavenly experience. For God promises that:

> "'What no eye has seen, what no ear has heard, and
> what no human mind has conceived'—the things God
> has prepared for those who love him."
>
> (1 Corinthians 2:9)

This is why everything was made. This is why we are here. This is what our lives are all about.

Think It Through! Talk It Over!
1. What three purposes do trials serve?
2. What has been your biggest trial? Do you believe God used that trial for your good? If so, why do you believe that?
3. Why, do you think, did God allow us to live in an imperfect world?
4. Why do you agree or disagree that most skeptics are unwilling to accept the truth about God because they do not want to be accountable to Him?
5. Why do you think God has chosen not to reveal everything to us about the afterlife?
6. Why do you agree or disagree with the statement that "every means God uses to persuade us never reaches the point of overcoming our ability to make free choices"?

7. What is there about this present life that makes you long for heaven?
8. What do see as the ultimate purpose of your life?
9. If we had all the answers to all our questions about what happens in this life and what lies beyond, would it be possible to have faith? Why or why not?
10. Are you glad that life on earth is just temporary? Why or why not?

Chapter 13

MY NEW LIFE

hen I began my investigation, I felt secure in my beliefs and my life as an atheist. No one has all the answers. But, from what I learned during my time in school and from independent reading, I felt confident that Darwin was correct. It also seemed that the way society operates supported this conclusion.

Having moved on from the debate about God and religion, I couldn't imagine discovering anything that would change my thinking. However, the more I read about most subjects the more I learned. So, I held out the possibility that I might uncover something during my investigation that would enhance what I already knew—more of a fill-in-the-details kind of thing rather than a game changer.

My approach to the investigation changed, however, when I started encountering scientific findings I never considered before. It began with the cosmos. I don't know why, but I'd never thought about how well-ordered nature is beginning with our own solar system. How could an entire system of various sized bodies randomly find themselves in the position we find them? How could each of the planets be the perfect size and move at just the right speed to maintain their perfect paths? The degree of precision was unfathomable. And this observation was hardly the beginning.

Although cosmology is what initially roused my interest, matters of biology soon followed. From our own bodies, to the structure of every living cell, one amazing fact after another caused me to realize that I was surrounded by a mass of information I'd never really considered before. Frankly, I was ashamed at my ignorance of it all. I felt like I was watching a door slowly open before me revealing a whole new world on the other side.

The more I discovered, the more my curiosity as well as my eagerness to learn more increased. What started as casual reading soon turned into intense research.

For months I continued to discover new facts both in the area of science as well as in the other subjects I was investigating. But the issues I was reading about seemed like random, disconnected electrons swirling around my head with new electrons frequently being added to the mix. I had always been an eager learner and enjoyed making new discoveries. However, for an extended period of time, I became frustrated because I wasn't able to connect many of the pieces.

Finally, I began to make connections between some of the parts I'd been investigating. One by one, the pieces began fitting together. Slowly, not only did I find that the evidence pointed to God's existence, but it also revealed His overall plan for us as His cherished creation. I started to see that many of the individual subjects I'd been studying were instruments used by God to offer us portions of His overall message.

My ability to make significant connections between the various subjects impacted me in an overwhelming way. As I continued to read night after night I sensed my thick hard shell softening. Then after arriving at my aha moment, I cracked. It took a week of reviewing the evidence before I felt confident that I wasn't just making something up. But no matter how many times I went through what I learned, I came to the same conclusion. After reevaluating the information and cross-examining myself over and over, the only thing remaining for me to do was to respect not only the facts, but their relationships to each other.

Though I prided myself on being observant, I was humbled that for so long I'd been misinterpreting so much of what was around me, some of which was staring me in the face every day. Up to this point of my life I'd been dogmatic in my mistaken beliefs, living in a way that was absent the essential truths of who we are as human beings. At the same time, however, I began feeling a growing sense of relief, excitement, and even joy that I'd acquired the fundamental understanding of who we are in light of God's existence. Knowing I had so much more to learn, I was comforted that I'd at least found the essential starting points.

I could see as I began looking back over the process of my investigation that my mindset of not wanting to be influenced or talked into something by others worked for my benefit. Performing my investigation alone helped me to pursue angles I might never have explored otherwise. If someone led me through the process, I might not have encountered the depth and richness of the facts that became so persuasive. Chasing down all the leads and going where each one led brought me to the large body of evidence that cornered me in the end.

All along, my investigation had been a highly analytical exercise. But now, significant emotional undertones began coming out as well. Though both shocked and overcome with joy from my discoveries, I was also sad. Instinctively, I knew that my extensive network of friends would view me differently. Having shared a common mindset with them on this polarizing issue, I strongly suspected that few, if any of these relationships would survive. Before telling my friends what I'd been up to I already felt alone. But despite the potential loss of these relationships, I could no longer claim ignorance to what I'd uncovered, nor did I want to. Suddenly, I was not the same person I was before. Yes, my choices were still mine. But now I was accountable for everything I'd learned.

So, after spending an additional week making sure I was as certain as possible about the facts and what they meant, I devoted some time to having my first conversations with my Creator. I asked Him to forgive me for my jaded attitude and stubborn denial of Him. I also asked Him to prepare me for what was about to happen. By nature I was a confident guy. But I knew that when I went public with what I'd been doing and announced the conclusions I'd reached, it would evoke strong reactions. So, I continued to read and talk to God for hours each evening. As I did so, I became stronger every day.

Finally, about two weeks later, the moment arrived. Not after a designated period of time, but just when I felt ready, I began telling everyone I knew what had happened. My predictions were amazingly accurate. My entire social structure collapsed in a matter of weeks. Only my close family stood by me. A shockwave seemed to go through the community. Part of the bewilderment and disbelief my friends experienced was because they weren't aware I'd been researching the issue of God's existence.

What did the future hold? I certainly didn't know the details. But I was confident that the truth I discovered would continue to transform me. At this point, I determined I needed to do something that was completely foreign to me. I knew it was important for me to seek out and embrace other believers—people who could guide me along this new journey.

I found it ironic that just a few months earlier I had scoffed at anything to do with "church." Before I began exploring matters of science and the Scriptures many of my evenings were spent socializing and drinking alcohol. I now found myself with a great desire to fill my time learning from people who lived as followers of God in accordance with the Scriptures.

I only casually knew of a few people who claimed to go to church regularly. Nonetheless, I didn't think it would be difficult to find believers. A number of churches were located on some of the busier streets in my area. Because the church I visited a couple times during my investigation was more than thirty minutes driving distance from where I lived, I chose instead to join the First Baptist Church of Merritt Island, the largest church in my area. It was just about a mile from my office building.

The extensive number of weekly activities First Baptist offered was a plus for me. I knew I needed to fill my now empty social calendar with activities that would help me further explore my new beliefs. I sensed there was much awaiting me and I couldn't wait to get started.

Soon after making this decision, I introduced myself to Larry Thompson, the man who'd serve as my first pastor. After summarizing for him all that had happened over the past few months, he flashed his patented huge smile, hugged me and said, "Welcome, brother."

END NOTES

Chapter 1

1   A 2007 LifeWay Research survey indicated 70% of those in their 20s who attended church in high school, stopped attending in college http://www.lifeway.com/article/?id=165949 (accessed October 28, 2011). In 2009, the American Research Group found that 89% of those attending church in high school left shortly after graduation. http://www.christianpost.com/article/20090629/survey-churches-losing-youths-long-before-college/index.html (accessed October 28, 2011).

Chapter 2

2   Brecher, Kenneth. "Galaxy" http://www.nasa.gov/worldbook/galaxy_worldbook.html (accessed November 11, 2010).

3   http://www.universetoday.com/25156/history-of-stars/ (accessed November 11, 2010).

4   http://www.nasa.gov/centers/kennedy/about/information/science_faq.html (accessed November 11, 2010).

5   http://nineplanets.org/sol.html (accessed November 11, 2010).

6   See generally Ross, Hugh. *The Creator and the Cosmos,* Third Edition. (Colorado Springs, CO., NavPress, 2001).

7   Newton, Sir Isaac. *The Mathematical Principals of Natural Philosophy,* Book III, (public domain).

8   http://www.windows2universe.org/our_solar_system/moons_table.html&edu=elem (accessed November 11, 2010).

9   Ross, Hugh. "Location, Location, Location! Research Reveals Fine-Tuning of the Solar System's Position" http://www.reasons.org/location-location-location-research-reveals-fine-tuning-solar-systems-position (accessed October 18, 2010).

10   http://www.nasa.gov/worldbook/earth_worldbook.html (accessed November 11, 2010).

11   http://www.astronomytoday.com/astronomy/earthmoon.html (accessed November 11, 2010).

12   http://oceanservice.noaa.gov/education/kits/tides/tides06_variations.html (accessed November 11, 2010).

13   From a lecture by Francis Collins: The Language of God: A Scientist Presents Evidence for Belief – California Institute of Technology, February 5, 2009. http://www.veritas.org/Media.aspx#/v/1 (accessed on November 14, 2010).
Read more explanations of DNA and other scientific perspectives by Francis Collins in his books:
The Language of Life: DNA and the Revolution in Personalized Medicine. (New York, NY., Harper, 2010) and
The Language of God: A Scientist Presents Evidence for Belief. (New York, NY., Free Press, 2007).

14   Meyer, Stephen C., *The Signature in the Cell: Evidence for Intelligent Design* (New York, NY., Harper Collins, 2009) and
Rana, Fuzale. *The Cell's Design: How Chemistry Reveals the Creator's Artistry* (Grand Rapids, MI., Baker Books, 2008).

15 http://vadim.oversigma.com/MAS862/Project.html (accessed November 11, 2010).

Chapter 3

16 Wright, N.T. *Simply Christian.* (New York, NY., Harper One (2006), 173-184. Also, http://www.allaboutthejourney.org/history-of-the-bible.htm (accessed October 28, 2011).

17 http://christiananswers.net/q-abr/abr-iraq.html (accessed January 3, 2014).

18 http://www.biblicalarchaeology.org/daily/ancient-cultures/ancient-near-eastern-world/the-last-days-of-hattusa/ (accessed January 3, 2014).

19 http://oi.uchicago.edu/research/projects/kho/ (accessed January 3, 2014).

20 Walvoord, John. *The Prophecy Knowledge Handbook.* (Wheaton, Ill., Victor Books, 1990), 10.

21 Ibid.

22 http://www.newworldencyclopedia.org/entry/Alexander_the_Great. (accessed January 4, 2014).

23 Augustine. *The City of God,* Modern Library Edition. (New York, NY., Random House, 1993), 343.

24 McDowell, Josh and McDowell, Sean. *Evidence For The Resurrection: What It Means For Your Relationship With God.* (Ventura, CA., Regal, 2009), 127-133.

25 Colson, Charles. *Loving God.* (Grand Rapid, MI., Zondervan Publishing, 1983), 57.

26 Lewis, Clive Staples. *Reflections on The Psalms.* (New York, NY., Harcourt, Inc., original copyright 1958 renewed 1986), 117-118.

Chapter 4

27   N. T. Wright. *Simply Christian: Why Christianity Makes Sense.* (New York, N.Y., Harper One, 2006), 106.

28   Blaise Pascal created a narrative summarizing many of the messianic prophesies recorded in *The Mind of Fire*, (Wheaton, Ill.,Victor Books, 2006), 191-193.

29   Bonhoffer, Dietrich. *The Cost of Discipleship.* (New York, NY., Touchstone Publishing, 1995), 205.

30   The daughter of Jairus – Mark 5:21-43; A young man from Nain – Luke 7:11-17; and Lazarus – John 11:1-44.

31   Mark 10:46-52; Matthew 20:29-34; Luke 18:35-43; and Matthew 9:27-31.

32   http://www.bcbsr.com/survey/jmrcls.html (accessed January 17, 2011).

Chapter 5

33   Graham, Billy. *Living In God's Love – The New York Crusade.* (New York, NY, Penguin Group, 2005), 31-32.

34   Ibid. p.27.

35   Taken from: Cheney, Johnston C.: *The Life of Christ in Stereo: The Four Gospels Speak in Harmony.* (Portland, OR. Multnomah Press, 1969), 140-141. This manuscript harmonizes the four Gospels into one chronological story without repeating any of the parts.

36   Also taken from: Cheney, Johnston C.: *The Life of Christ in Stereo: The Four Gospels Speak in Harmony.* (Portland, OR. Multnomah Press, 1969), 55-56.

37   Wright, N.T. *Simply Christian: Why Christianity Makes Sense.* (New York, N.Y., Harper One, 2006), 107.

38   Colson, Charles. *The Faith.* (Grand Rapids, MI., Zondervan, 2008), 90-91.

39   Lucado, Max. *He Chose The Nails.* (Nashville, TN., Thomas Nelson, 2000), 33-34.

40   Keller, Timothy. *The Reason For God.* (New York, N.Y., Riverhead Books, 2008), 192,187.

Chapter 6

41   Gen. 3:16-17.

42   Lewis, Clive Staples. *The Problem of Pain.* (New York, N.Y., Macmillan Publishing Company, 1962), 93.

43   Ehrman, Bart. *God's Problem: How the Bible Fails to Answer Our Most Important Question – Why We Suffer.* (New York, N.Y., Harper One, 2008).

44   Pascal, Blaise. *Penses,* Part 2 - Section 72

Chapter 7

45   Lewis, Clive Staples. *Mere Christianity.* (New York, N.Y., MacMillan Publishing Company, 1943), 163.

46   http://www.logoslibrary.org/tertullian/apology/39.html (accessed February 2, 2014).

47   See also Paul's more expansive explanation of how the Church functions in 1 Corinthians 12:12-27.

48   Colson, Charles and Ellen Vaughn. *Being The Body.* (Nashville, TN.,W Publishing Group, a division of Thomas Nelson, 2003), 26.

49   Ibid. p.10-11.

Chapter 8

50   Emily Charles@KimikoKrash (accessed 4-26-13) (pic.twitter)

51   Dennett, Daniel C. *Consciousness Explained, (Boston, Little, Brown and Company, Boston, 1991), 21-22.*

52   Genesis 1:26.

53 By example, Paul used his reasoning skills to present the truth to others. (Act 17:2-3; 18:19)

54 http://www.coptic.net/articles/ClementOfAlexandria.txt (accessed on November 12, 2010).

55 Keller, Timothy. *The Reason for God* (New York, N.Y., Riverhead Books, published by the Penguin Group, 2008), 152.

56 Ibid. p.163.

57 In many different ways, the Scriptures refer to or address the fact that we are emotional beings. In Genesis 43:30 and 2 Samuel 18:33, the Scriptures describe situations in which people were "overcome with emotion." Also, Proverbs 16:32 refers to the need to "control" our emotions.

58 Keller, Timothy. *The Reason for God.* (New York, N.Y., Riverhead Books, published by the Penguin Group, 2008), 70.

Chapter 9

59 Graham, William. *Hope For The Troubled Heart*, (Dallas, TX., Word Publishing, 1991), 216.

60 I also gained my understanding about this situation from Matthew 22:1-10 and Luke 14:15-24.

Chapter 10

61 A 20th-Century Master Scam, Article. The New York Times. July 18, 1999. http://www.nytimes.com/1999/07/18/magazine/a-20th-century-master-scam.html?pagewanted=all&src=pm

62 Ibid.

63 Lewis, Clive Staples. *The Screwtape Letters.* (Grand Rapids, MI., Baker Book House Company, 1975).

64 Swindoll, Charles. *Job Interactive Study Guide.* (Dallas, TX.,W Publishing Group, 2004), 6.

65   Omartian, Stormie. *The Power of a Praying Parent.* (Eugene, OR., Harvest House Publishers, 1995), 63.

Chapter 11

66   1 John 4:7-21.

67   McDonald, George. *Discovering The Character of God* (Compiled, Arranged, and Edited by Michael R. Phillips) (Bloomington, MN., Bethany House Publishers, 1989), 29.

Chapter 12

68   In the early passages in Job we read how Satan operates under certain limitations and needs permission to go beyond them. Satan is a created being and doesn't hold the same power as his Creator.

SPECIAL THANKS:

I've been greatly blessed in this life. The most recent additions to that long list include the wonderful people who've helped this book come to be.

First on my list to thank is my wife, Nichole. She's the first to read my words and provide so many great suggestions. Likewise to my children—Cody, Grace, Emily, and Joshua—for their patience while dad as been writing over the last few years. Thanks also to Terry Burns, my wonderful agent, Jim Dyet, an awesome editor, to Steve Martens, Hugh Jones, Scoti Domeij, Beth Vogt, and Karen Pickering for their support of me and their unique contributions to this work. A special thanks also to the wonderful editorial team at Morgan James including, David Hancock, Terry Whalin, Margo Tolouse, Bethany Marshal, and Jim Howard.

I am so grateful.

ABOUT MICHAEL

For more information about Michael and to explore his resources, please visit: michaelminot.com.

You can also dialog with Michael and read his daily posts on Twitter at @MichaelMinot.

If you're interested in booking Michael for a speaking engagement at your church, university, or high school please see Michael's speaking page on his website.

Interested in interviewing Michael for your TV or radio show, for an article or as part of your book review? You may schedule time with Michael by using the link on michaelminot.com.

PERMISSION TO USE

Please feel free to use up to 200 words without my permission. If used during a presentation such as a church service, please reference the book and author using the same font size as follows:

The Beckoning: Examining The Truths That Transformed An Atheist Attorney Into A Believer In God by Michael Minot, Page _____.